Stick Figuring through the Bible

New Testament Overview

A Chronological Study of the Major Characters and Events of the New Testament

Teacher Edition

Level 1-2

Grapevine Studies
P.O. Box 2123
Glenrock, WY 82637
(877) 436-2317

Web site: www.grapevinestudies.com

Email: info@grapevinestudies.com

New Testament Overview
Level 1-2
Teacher Edition

By Dianna Wiebe

Copyright 2005 by Grapevine Studies

ISBN 1-59873-012-6

All rights reserved. No part of this work may be reproduced or used in any form, by any means--graphic, electronic, or mechanical including: photocopying, recording, taping, or information storage and retrieval systems--without written permission from the author.

All scripture quotations, unless otherwise indicated, are taken from the New King James Version®. Copyright 1982 by Thomas Nelson, Inc. Used by permission. All rights reserved.

Maps are courtesy of Steven Gordon at Cartagram LLC, www.cartagram.com

Cover design by Sean Athey of Profession Print Management, www.proprintman.com.

New Testament Overview

Level 1-2

Dedication

This lesson series is dedicated to our children--Cody, Tabitha, Luke and Zak. Isaiah 59:21

We would also like to dedicate this book to all those parents and teachers who desire to diligently teach their children and their students the Word of God.

Acknowledgements

I would first like to thank the Lord God Almighty for His faithfulness to me through the years to me. The inspiration, the creativity, and the ideas for this study have all come from Him.

I would like to thank my beloved husband, John, for his spiritual leadership and oversight of this large project, for his prayers, advice, encouragement, and support! If he hadn't laughed and loved my first stick-figured lessons, I never would have attempted this book!

Thank you Dave and Janet Bowman, for boldly teaching what no one had taught before! Thank you for piloting this program with me--you have given me great advice and been a great encouragement!

Thank you Brian and Kim Peil for your constant encouragement--you've taught me what determination means.

A special thank you goes to Mary Jo Tate for editing our books--it has been a pleasure to work with you on this project.

The Inspiration

Matthew 22:36-40

"Teacher, which is the great commandment in the law?" Jesus said to him, "'You shall love the Lord your God with all your heart, with all your soul, and with all your mind.' This is the first and greatest commandment. And the second is like it: 'You shall love your neighbor as yourself.' On these two commandments hang all the Law and the Prophets."

Galatians 4:4-5

But when the fullness of the time had come, God sent forth His Son, born of a woman, born under the law, to redeem those who were under the law, that we might receive the adoption as sons.

Table of Contents

THE GRAPEVINE MISSION	VIII
THE GRAPEVINE METHOD	VIII
THE GRAPEVINE STUDIES	IX
STATEMENT OF FAITH	IX
GRAPEVINE TEACHER GOALS	X
GRAPEVINE STUDENT GOALS	X
TEACHER AND STUDENT SUPPLY LIST	X
TEACHING GRAPEVINE LESSONS	XI
SECTION 1 GOALS AND KEY POINTS	**2**
NEW TESTAMENT TIMELINE NARRATIVE	2
NEW TESTAMENT TIMELINE	9
SECTION 2 GOALS AND KEY POINTS	**22**
BIRTH OF JOHN	28
BIRTH OF JESUS	31
HEROD AND THE WISE MEN	37
JESUS AT THE TEMPLE	43
JOHN BAPTIZED JESUS	49
REVIEW 1	54
SECTION 3 GOALS AND KEY POINTS	**56**
THE TEMPTATION OF JESUS	59
SATAN	65
THE TWELVE APOSTLES	71
JESUS TAUGHT	77
JESUS PRAYED	83
JESUS AND THE SEA	89
REVIEW 2	94
SECTION 4 GOALS AND KEY POINTS	**96**
JESUS FED THE MULTITUDES	99
JESUS HEALED THE SICK	105
JESUS HEALED THE DEMON-POSSESSED	111
JESUS RAISED THE DEAD	117
JESUS ENTERED JERUSALEM	123
THE LAST SUPPER	129
REVIEW 3	134
MID-SERIES REVIEW	**137**
SECTION 5 GOALS AND KEY POINTS	**144**
THE LAST SUPPER	**146**
THE GARDEN OF GETHSEMANE	147
THE TRIALS OF JESUS	153
JESUS WAS CONDEMNED TO DEATH	162

THE CRUCIFIXION	165
THE DEATH OF JESUS	174
THE BURIAL AND RESURRECTION	177
REVIEW 4	182

SECTION 6 GOALS AND KEY POINTS 184

THE ASCENSION	187
WAS JESUS THE MESSIAH? (PART 1)	193
WAS JESUS THE MESSIAH? (PART 2)	199
THE HOLY SPIRIT	205
THE EARLY CHURCH	211
THE PERSECUTION	217
REVIEW 5	222

SECTION 7 GOALS AND KEY POINTS 224

SAUL	232
PAUL	238
LETTERS TO THE CHURCHES (PART 1)	239
LETTERS TO THE CHURCHES (PART 2)	245
THE GOSPEL IN STICK FIGURES	251
SHARING THE GOSPEL	257
REVIEW 6	262

SECTION 8 GOALS AND KEY POINTS 264

THE SEALS, TRUMPETS, AND BOWLS (PART 1)	267
THE SEALS, TRUMPETS, AND BOWLS (PART 2)	273
THE SECOND COMING OF JESUS	279
HELL	285
HEAVEN	291
REVIEW 7	297

FINAL REVIEW 299

ADDENDUM 311

THE APOSTLE'S CREED	313
NOTES FOR THE APOSTLE'S CREED	314
WEEKLY SCHEDULE	315
WEEKLY SCHEDULE NOTES	316
DAILY SCHEDULE	317

The Grapevine Mission

Our mission at Grapevine Studies is to provide believers with a method and curriculums to study the Bible, using a timeline, stick figures, words, symbols, and colors to teach chronological lessons.

The Grapevine Method

Grapevine Studies teaches the Bible as if it were a puzzle, doing the frame first. Once the framework is in place (the timeline) then individual pieces (Bible passages, characters, and events) are much easier to place and understand in the context of the "whole puzzle" (the whole counsel of the Word of God).

This lesson series will first introduce and teach the New Testament timeline. Each subsequent lesson will begin with a **timeline review** up to the point of that day's lesson. As students **read** the Bible lessons they will be able to place their "puzzle pieces" into their framework (timeline) and have an understanding of the context of the character/event they are reading about. Students read passages from the Bible and **draw** (or take notes on) each section of Scripture, using what we at Grapevine Studies call **stick figuring**. Stick figuring is using stick figures, symbols, colors, charts, and words to illustrate each Bible passage. This method allows students to interact with the Bible passage and be as creative as they desire. At the end of each lesson a set of **review questions** is given to ensure that students have grasped the essentials of the passage (the who, what, where, when, why, and how). **Application** of the lesson is for the teacher to determine based upon prayer, the class, the needs of individual students, and what that teacher feels the Lord has led him to emphasize. Each lesson ends with a Bible **memory verse** that is related to the lesson and the timeline.

The *New Testament Overview* ends with a review of the series' timeline and memory verses. By the end of this series your student should be able to complete the entire New Testament timeline alone. In addition, students should know several facts regarding each character and event they have studied and know where the books of the Bible fit into the timeline. Students will also be very familiar with using Bible study tools including, a topical Bible, Bible concordance, and Bible dictionary.

Our prayer is that those who take this journey, both teachers and students, will expand in their knowledge of the Bible and grow in their love for the Lord and His Word. May God bless you richly as you study and teach His Word!

2005

The Grapevine Studies Statement of Faith

Bible: We believe that the Bible is the inspired, infallible, authoritative, complete Word of God and is accurate in all historical and scientific references.

God: We believe that there is one holy and perfect God, externally existent in three persons—Father, Son, and Holy Spirit.

Jesus: We believe that Jesus Christ is true God and true man; in His virgin birth, sinless life, miracles, atoning death, bodily resurrection, ascension, and in His physical return.

Holy Spirit: We believe that the Holy Spirit is the divine third person of the triune God, sent to indwell, comfort, teach, empower the believer; and to convict the unbeliever of sin.

Man: We believe man was originally created perfect, in the image and likeness of God, with an unbroken relationship to God. When the first man (Adam) disobeyed God, the perfect relationship that God and man was broken and the curse of sin and death entered all creation. All men are born with this sin nature and only the atoning work of the Lord Jesus Christ can remove man's sinful nature and restore the broken relationship with God.

Salvation: We believe that salvation (forgiveness of sin against God) is provided only through faith in the life, death, resurrection, and ascension of Jesus Christ for all me who believe, repent, and receive the gift of eternal life. As a result of faith, works will follow.

Resurrection: We believe in the resurrection of both the believer (saved) and the unbeliever (unsaved); the believer to eternal life and the unbeliever to eternal damnation.

Teacher-Directed Doctrine

Grapevine Studies is please to be able to provide Bible curriculum to a variety of denominations. Our unique teacher-directed doctrinal approach provides a platform for each teacher/parent to explain their specific doctrines as they come up with in each lesson.

2005

Grapevine Teacher Goals

Grapevine Studies assumes that teachers of this curriculum will already have a personal and intimate relationship with the Lord, and a calling to teach the Word of God. At Grapevine Studies our goals for teachers are that you will:

- Learn more of the character of the God you serve and His word.
- Be godly examples to your students.
- Effectively communicate the Word of God to this generation of believers.
- Instruct only after having spent time in prayer, Bible reading, and study.
- Have sufficient preparation time for your own study without the need to gather, order, and put together multiple supplies for various activities.
- Learn along with your students.

Grapevine Student Goals

Grapevine Studies believes that students who are taught using reading, hearing, and drawing will have a higher retention rate then those who are just lectured. We also believe that teaching the Bible in a chronological and sequential format is the best for long-term memory and life impact At Grapevine Studies our goals for students are that they will:

- Be introduced to the One that all history pointed toward—Jesus, the Messiah, The Christ. Once students become believers, to teach them to know God and live a holy life.

- See God's interaction and movement through history as He dealt with nations and individuals so that they will be able to recognize God's interaction and movement in their own lives.

- Have a framework of the Bible that will encourage and inspire them to study further on their own, to fill in their own Biblical puzzle, and to understand the context of the passages they read in the future.

- Practice using various Bible study tools: topical Bible, concordance, and Bible dictionary.

- Learn from those who have lived before us.

Teacher and Student Supply List

- Teacher supplies: a Bible, Grapevine Studies Teacher Guide, a dry erase board, dry erase markers of various colors, wall maps, a topical Bible, concordance, and a Bible dictionary.

- Student supplies: a Bible, Grapevine Studies Student Book, pencil or pen, colored pencils, a topical Bible, concordance, and a Bible dictionary.

Teaching Grapevine Lessons

Before Class

Prayer: Nothing can replace the time a teacher spends with our Master Teacher, the Lord God Almighty.

Section Goals and Key Points: As you prepare for your lesson, I recommend a review of the lesson goals and key points at the beginning of each section. These pages are designed to give you a concise summary of the lesson you will be teaching.

Research Links: We have provided research links on our website to aid you in your study. Our website is www.grapevinestudies.com/Links.htm.

Schedule

Weekly (Bible Study or Sunday School Class)

We recommend one lesson each week. Class time can be used to review answers to questions on the Review Page, give presentations of the Activities and Further Study assignments. For a year long study, the fifty lessons included in your book will allow two extra weeks to complete any assignments or to have free for holidays or special events. See Addendum for Weekly Schedule.

Daily (School)

We recommend one page of each lesson, per day, for a complete school year. See Addendum for Daily Schedule.

> Day 1: Timeline and memory verse review page.
>
> Day 2: Complete page one of the lesson.
>
> Day 3: Complete page two of the lesson.
>
> Day 4: Create the character and event card and review their memory verse for that lesson. Level 2 students will also continue with their memory work found at the bottom of the page.

The Timeline

Lesson 1 of this series is an overview of the Old Testament timeline. I have written the teacher notes in such a way that you could read them to your students and then draw each character or event on the board. I recommend that you read over it and become familiar enough with it that you can tell the story in your own words. Remember that this is not a detailed lesson but an overview of the coming year. Throughout the year we will examine each character and event in more detail.

2005

Review Page

The goal of this page is to review the timeline and the memory verses from the past three lessons.

Timeline Review: Students will draw in the pictures on the timeline and fill in the missing titles below the timeline. Teacher's editions have the pictures drawn in and the missing titles.

Memory Verses: Students will review the previous three memory verses by either writing out the entire verse or filling in the missing words.

Lesson Pages

Background Bible Reading: This is required reading for teachers. Some lessons encompass a great deal of information that cannot be covered in a single lesson. Teachers will need to determine what information they might want to "fill in" to make the lesson as understandable as possible for their students.

Time Frame: The time frame gives students the context of the lesson.

Section Titles: These titles correspond with the student lessons.

Teacher Notes: The teacher notes, in italic print, explain the important information that will need to be covered in that section of the lesson. These notes will also be helpful for substitute teachers and can even be read to the students if needed. Space has been provided in each section for you to write in your own notes.

Student Pages: Student page (SP) numbers are found in the box at the lower right hand corner of corresponding pages.

Level 1 and Level 2: This combined teacher manual will enable you to teach both levels from one book. Notes, drawings, review questions, and answers are the same for both levels.

Look-up Words: This symbol indicates the words that I recommend you look up. This may mean simply looking up the word in a Bible dictionary or *Strong's Concordance*, but it may also mean doing some further research so that you know the function of that word. For example, the word for "priest", your students will need more than just a definition. For priest, you will want them to know where the priest served, the duties a priest performed, why the priests were important, etc. This will allow your students to better understand the context of the passage you are studying, while enabling you to answer questions that might arise regarding these words. All look-up words are from the New King James Version of the Bible, if you are using a different version of the Bible your look-up words may vary slightly.

2005

Draw: This is to give you a written description of what I have drawn on lesson pages of the teacher notes. Color choices are up to the teacher and student. We suggest that you use only the color purple to represent God, Jesus Christ, and the Holy Spirit.

Review Questions and Answers: This section gives you the questions and answers for the lesson review. Answers may vary. Please note that the last question of each lesson is "What do we learn about God from these verses?" This is the application question of the lesson. The answer to this question will depend upon what the Lord has led you to emphasize. My answers reflect the way in which I have taught that lesson, but may not be how the Lord will lead you to teach the lesson.

Teaching the Lessons

Reading: Following the short review which will set the time frame for the lesson, the first set of Scriptures will be read (see first Scripture box). If you are teaching Level 1 and Level 2 students at the same time we recommend using the Level 4 scripture readings. If you are teaching only Level 1 students, we recommend using the student edition as a guide for scripture readings.

Drawing: After the Scripture is read, the teacher will then stick figure that portion of Scripture onto the board. Students can either draw what the teacher has drawn or their own interpretation of the Scripture section. I encourage colors and creativity. Some students may opt to take notes in this section.

Lesson Review: At the end of the lesson there will be a lesson review. These questions will cover the who, what, when, where, why, and how of the lesson. Teachers are encouraged to ask additional questions as needed for comprehension and review.

Memory Verse: A memory verse is given at the end of each lesson that will relate to the lesson and the timeline.

Character and Event Cards

Character and Event Cards: On Day 4 of each lesson student will make their Character and Event Cards and review their memory verse. These cards are designed to be memory aids and used for reviews. On the front of each card students will write the title of that card, i.e. Creation. On the back of each card you will have your students put the information you want them to remember about each character or event. If you are teaching Level 2, memory work is included at the bottom of this page.

2005

Reviews

The goal of the reviews is to show the students what they **have learned**. There are five types of reviews built into this curriculum:

1. Timeline Review: the timeline or a section of the timeline is reviewed at the beginning of each lesson.

2. Lesson Review: at the end of each class.

3. Section Reviews: after each section, every five to six lessons. Each section ends with a review that covers a sampling of the lesson review questions and all the memory verses from that section. There are many ways to do this review without writing out the answer to each question. Be creative!

    - Trivia: Divide the class into two groups or challenge another class to a trivia game using the review questions.

    - Matching: Put the questions and answers on individual pieces of paper and then match them.

4. Mid-Series Review: at the mid-point of the series. This review covers the timeline and the memory verses to date.

5. Final Review: at the end of the series. The final review covers the Old Testament timeline and all the memory verses from this series. The final review is designed to show students how much of the Old Testament they have learned.

The New Testament Narrative

Section 1 Goals and Key Points

NEW TESTAMENT TIMELINE NARRATIVE

The goal of this lesson is to give the students the outline for the entire lesson series. You will draw the timeline on the board while the students draw it on their notebook sheets. The following key points are a brief explanation of the facts you will want to communicate to your students. As a teacher you will want to become familiar with the key points of the timeline so that you are teaching the timeline in your own words.

Key points:

Adam: The Old Testament begins with the account of the creation week. On the sixth day God created the first man, Adam. Adam was created to have a perfect and complete relationship with God. When Adam sinned, by disobeying God, and ate the forbidden fruit, the relationship between God and man was broken. However, God promised Adam that one day the Messiah would come, would be born of a woman, and would restore the broken relationship between God and man.

Noah: Ten generations after Adam, Noah was born and lived. Noah built the ark and survived the Flood.

Abraham: Ten generations after Noah, God made a covenant with Abraham, telling him that the coming Messiah would be born through his family line.

David: Fourteen generations after Abraham, a descendant of Abraham named David was born. David was the second king of Israel, and God promised him that through his family line the Messiah would come.

Captivity in Babylon: Fourteen generations after David lived, the captivity of Judah took place.

Jesus: Fourteen generations after the captivity in Babylon, the Messiah was born according to promise.

The Eyes: Throughout the Old Testament, our eyes looked forward to the Messiah, the One who would (1) be born of woman, (2) be born of the line of Abraham, and (3) be born of the line of David.

Birth of John: The first chronological event of the New Testament is the birth of John (commonly known as John the Baptist). An angel announced to Zacharias that he and his barren wife, Elizabeth, would have a son named John. Zacharias was told that John would be the man who would prepare the people for the coming Messiah.

Birth of Jesus: The Old Testament had pointed to the coming Messiah, and the time had come for Him to be born (Galatians 4:4-5). The angel Gabriel appeared to a virgin named Mary to announce that she had been chosen by God to be the mother of the Messiah. Mary lived in Nazareth and was betrothed to man named Joseph. An angel appeared to Joseph, and a short time later Joseph and Mary married and traveled to Bethlehem, where Jesus was born. The angel announced Jesus' birth to the shepherds in the fields and they traveled to Bethlehem to see the newborn baby. When Jesus was eight days old He was circumcised, and at forty days old He was presented in the temple, according to the Law. Our eyes at this time begin to look down, watching the Messiah who has come.

Jesus in Egypt: Wise men from the East, who had followed a star, also came to worship Jesus. When the wise men arrived in Judea seeking to worship the newborn king of the Jews, the current king, Herod, was upset by their announcement and subsequent escape. Seeking to kill Jesus, Herod ordered the death of all children age two and under living in and around Bethlehem. An angel told Joseph to take Mary and Jesus away, and the family escaped Herod's order by moving to Egypt, where they remained until the death of Herod. After Herod's death Joseph returned with his family, and they settled in a town called Nazareth.

Jesus at Age Twelve: Little is recorded about Jesus' childhood except that at age twelve He went with His family to attend the Feast of Passover in Jerusalem in accordance with the Law.

John Prepared the Way: John grew up and lived in the wilderness until the time came for him to prepare the people for the coming Messiah. John preached in the wilderness of Judea, telling the people to repent, and he baptized those who repented. Later John was put into prison by Herod the Tetrarch (King Herod's son) and beheaded.

The Baptism of Jesus: As John became well known in the area, people asked if he was the Messiah. John clearly stated that he was not the Messiah but had only been sent to prepare the people for Him. Jesus went to the Jordan River, where John was baptizing, and asked John to baptize Him. As John baptized Jesus, God the Father spoke from heaven in an audible voice, and the Holy Spirit descended in the form of a dove. Jesus was about thirty years old at this time.

The Temptation of Jesus: Immediately after Jesus was baptized, the Holy Spirit led Jesus into the wilderness, where He fasted for forty days and nights. At the end of the fast, Satan came to tempt Jesus; Jesus responded to every temptation with the words, "It is written." Although Jesus was tempted throughout His lifetime, He never sinned. After Jesus was tempted angels, came and ministered to Him.

The Twelve Apostles: Once Jesus left the wilderness, He began to preach and many disciples began to follow Him. After a night of prayer Jesus chose twelve of His disciples and made them apostles.

At this point in the timeline we will be taking a look at the ministry of Jesus, covering approximately three years. Instead of looking at each individual event, we will group major events together.

Jesus Taught: Many times throughout the ministry of Jesus we read that He was teaching. Jesus taught His apostles, His disciples, and many others.

Jesus Prayed: Many passages refer to Jesus praying. The words used to describe Jesus at prayer are: alone, often, all night, and the Father's will.

Jesus and the Sea: One of the many miracles that Jesus performed was the calming of the sea in the midst of a storm. When Jesus spoke, Creation responded. After Jesus calmed the storm, His disciples marveled at what He had done and questioned among themselves who He was. At another point in Jesus' ministry, He also walked on water.

Jesus Fed the Multitudes: Jesus showed that He was concerned not only with the spiritual lives of those who sought to learn from Him but also their physical lives. Scripture records two separate accounts where Jesus fed multitudes, one time feeding 5,000 men (not including women and children) and one time feeding 7,000 men.

Jesus Healed the Sick/Lame: Many times throughout Jesus' ministry He healed people of various physical ailments. Jesus healed the deaf, the dumb, the blind, the mute, the lepers, and the lame.

Jesus Healed the Demon-Possessed: In addition to the physical healings, Jesus also healed those who were demon-possessed. Many times Jesus cast out demons that had possessed and tormented men, women, and children. It is interesting to note that the demons knew that Jesus was the Messiah and that Jesus often commanded them to keep silent.

Jesus Raised the Dead: Although Jesus performed many miracles during His ministry, few compared with the people that Jesus raised from the dead. At the end of Jesus' time of ministry, He raised Lazarus from the dead after he had been in the tomb for four days. Word of Lazarus's resurrection by Jesus caused many Jews to believe that He was indeed the Messiah. Lazarus's resurrection also caused the unbelieving Jewish leaders to begin plotting to kill both Lazarus and Jesus.

Jesus Entered Jerusalem: Jesus entered Jerusalem with His disciples to celebrate the Feast of Passover and to begin the last week of His earthly life. Jesus rode into Jerusalem on a donkey, and the people waved leafy branches and shouted "Hosanna." This event is celebrated by Christians today on Palm Sunday. During this week Jesus went to the temple, removed the moneychangers, healed the sick, and taught. Also, during this week Judas began to plot with the chief priest, who sought to arrest and kill Jesus.

The Last Supper: At the Last Supper Jesus washed His apostles' feet and warned them of His coming death, telling them that they would all betray Him. After the meal Judas left, and Jesus instructed the eleven regarding the bread and the wine and New Covenant. After the meal Jesus and the eleven sang and then departed to the Garden of Gethsemane.

The Garden of Gethsemane: Arriving at the garden, Jesus asked Peter, James, and John to go a little further into the garden with Him to pray. The apostles repeatedly fell asleep while Jesus prayed with such intensity that His sweat was as blood. Jesus' prayer during this time in the garden was that the Father's will would be done.

Jesus Arrested: The chief priest, the Pharisees, and Roman troops found Jesus in the garden, and there Judas betrayed Him. When Jesus was arrested, the eleven Apostles fled.

Jesus Put on Trial: After Jesus was arrested He was put on trial. Throughout the night and into the morning Jesus endured six individual trials, three religious and three civil. After Jesus was beaten and scourged, Pilate condemned Him to death by crucifixion.

Jesus Crucified: At approximately 9:00 in the morning, Jesus was crucified between two thieves with a sign over His head reading, "Jesus, the King of the Jews." At about 3:00 in the afternoon, Jesus died. At the time of Jesus' death there were many amazing events: darkness and earthquake, the temple veil was torn top to bottom, and graves were opened and those who had been dead appeared to many.

Jesus Died and Was Buried: After a Roman soldier verified that Jesus was indeed dead, He was taken down from the cross and buried in the borrowed tomb of Joseph of Arimathea.

Jesus Rose from the Dead: After three days Jesus conquered death and the grave by rising from the dead. On the third day when the women went to the tomb to anoint Jesus' body, an angel met them and told them of His resurrection. (It is at this point that I complete the Gospel, drawing the broken relationship between God and man being restored by Jesus' sacrifice on the cross.)

Jesus Appeared for Forty Days: After Jesus' resurrection He appeared many times and to many people, at one time appearing to a crowd numbering 500. Jesus met with His apostles on different occasions, verifying His resurrection and giving them final instructions.

Jesus Ascended: At the end of forty days Jesus ascended to heaven, where He now sits at the right hand of the Father interceding for us. An angel appeared to the apostles when Jesus ascended and told them that when He returns, He will come in the same manner.

The Holy Spirit Given: Fifty days after Jesus died on the cross, on the Feast of Pentecost, the disciples were gathered in an upper room in Jerusalem as Jesus had commanded them. While they were praying the Holy Spirit came upon them in the form of tongues of fire.

The Eyes: Beginning with this page we will have two sets of eyes, one set looking back to what Jesus, the Messiah, did while He was on earth and the second set of eyes looking forward to His return.

The Early Church: On the day of Pentecost, the day the Holy Spirit was given to the Church, Peter preached at the temple, and 3,000 men believed and were baptized. Many things marked the early, Church including prayer, fellowship, the breaking of bread together, and following the apostles' teachings.

The Persecution Began: Not long after the birth of the Church, the persecution of those who accepted Jesus as the Messiah began. The first man to die because of his faith in Jesus the Messiah was Stephen, was tried and stoned to death. Many others believers were also arrested and imprisoned during this time.

Saul/Paul: While Stephen was being stoned a young man named Saul watched the coats of those doing the stoning. Saul became an aggressive persecutor of the followers of Jesus. While Saul was traveling to Damascus to persecute believers, he encountered Jesus and became a believer himself. God changed Saul's name to Paul, and through Paul the gospel spread to the Gentiles.

Letters to the Churches: Many of the books of the New Testament are letters written to Churches established by the eleven apostles and Paul. These letters cover a great number of topics related to living the Christian life.

The Gospel Spreads: After the giving of the Holy Spirit, the Church continued to grow and will eventually spread throughout the world.

Teacher Note: There is much debate about the events recorded in the book of Revelation. I have purposely left this timeline as open as we can to enable you, the teacher, to give your perspective on the events recorded in this book.

The Great Tribulation: There is a time of great tribulation marked by three judgments: the seven seal judgments, seven trumpet judgments, and the seven bowl judgments.

Jesus Returns: At the end of the great tribulation, Jesus will return.

The Millennium: At the beginning of the millennium, Satan will be chained to the bottomless pit and will be unchained at the end of the millennium. The millennium is a 1,000-year period of time in which Jesus reigns sovereign.

The White Throne Judgment: At the white throne judgment, all mankind will stand before God and be judged.

Hell: Hell was originally designed as a place of judgment of the devil and his angels, but it will also contain those who have rejected Jesus the Messiah.

Heaven: Heaven awaits believers in Jesus the Messiah and will be a place where God dwells among His people.

My Notes on the Timeline:

My Notes on the Timeline:

The New Testament Timeline

Lesson 1
Level 1-2

New Testament Timeline

10	10	14	14	14

Adam — Noah — Abraham — David — Babylon / Captivity in Babylon — Jesus

62 Generations between Adam and Jesus

Grapevine Studies
New Testament

Lesson 1
Level 1-2

New Testament Timeline

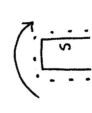

Nazareth

| Birth of John | Birth of Jesus | Jesus in Egypt | Jesus at Age Twelve | Passover |

SP 3

2005
11

Grapevine Studies
New Testament

Lesson 1
Level 1-2

New Testament Timeline

| John Prepared the Way | The Baptism of Jesus | Temptation of Jesus | The Twelve Apostles |

SP 4

Grapevine Studies
New Testament

Lesson 1
Level 1-2

New Testament Timeline

| Jesus Taught | Jesus Prayed | Jesus Calmed the Sea | Jesus Fed the Multitudes |

SP 5

2005

Grapevine Studies
New Testament

Lesson 1
Level 1-2

New Testament Timeline

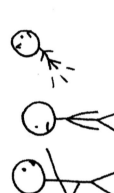

Jesus Healed the Sick/Lame | Jesus Healed the Demon-Possessed | Jesus Raised the Dead

Grapevine Studies
New Testament

Lesson 1
Level 1-2

New Testament Timeline

Jesus Entered Jerusalem

The Last Supper

The Garden of Gethsemane

SP 7

Grapevine Studies
New Testament

Lesson 1
Level 1-2

New Testament Timeline

| Jesus Was Arrested | Jesus Tried and Condemned | Jesus Was Crucified | Jesus Died and Was Buried |

3 Religious
3 Civil

SP 8

Grapevine Studies
New Testament

Lesson 1
Level 1-2

New Testament Timeline

Jesus Rose from the Dead

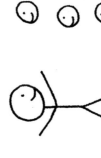
Jesus Appeared for Forty Days

Jesus Ascended

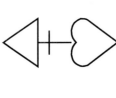

SP 9

17

2005

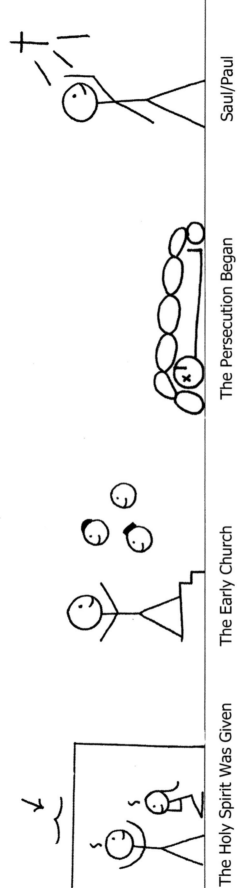

Grapevine Studies
New Testament

Lesson 1
Level 1-2

New Testament Timeline

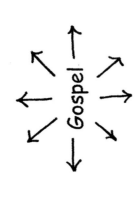

| Letters to the Churches | The Gospel Spreads | The Great Tribulation |

7 Seal Judgments
7 Trumpet Judgments
7 Bowl Judgments

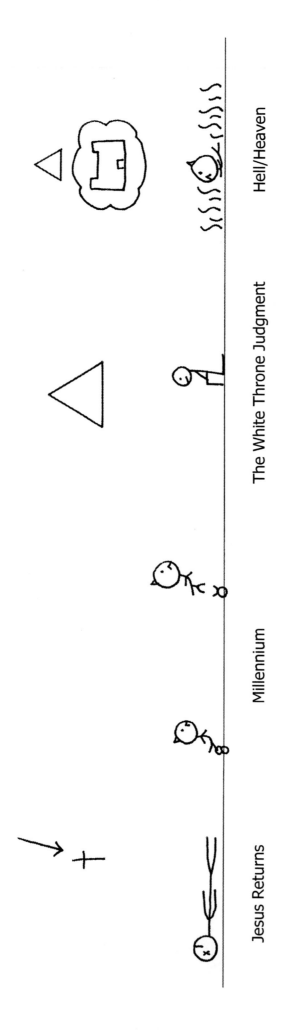

Section 2 Goals and Key Points

BIRTH OF JOHN

The goal of this lesson is for the students to be introduced to John (the Baptist).

Key Points:
- Zacharias and Elizabeth were righteous people but had no children.
- The angel Gabriel appeared to Zacharias in the temple, announcing that he and Elizabeth would have a son.
- Zacharias was struck mute for disbelief until John was named.
- Zacharias prophesied that John would prepare the way for the Messiah.
- John grew up strong in spirit and lived in the desert until it was time for him to prepare the children of Israel for their coming Messiah.

BIRTH OF JESUS

The goal of this lesson is for the students to see that in the fullness of time God sent His Son into the world.

Key Points:
- The angel Gabriel announced to Mary, a virgin from Nazareth, that she would be the mother of the Messiah.
- After Gabriel spoke to Joseph, Joseph took Mary as his wife.
- Joseph and Mary travel to Bethlehem to be registered.
- The Messiah, Jesus the Christ, was born in Bethlehem!
- Angels announced to shepherds the birth of Messiah.
- The shepherds worshiped Jesus.
- Joseph and Mary took Jesus to the temple, where both Simon and Anna prophesied over Him.

HEROD AND THE WISE MEN

The goal of this lesson is for the students to learn some of the facts about events that surrounded the early years of Jesus' earthly life.

Key Points:
- The wise men had traveled from the East in order to worship the newborn king of the Jews.
- Herod sought to find Jesus.
- The wise men found Jesus, worshipped Him, and presented Him with gifts.
- Herod attempted to kill Jesus by having all the male children two years old and younger living in and around Bethlehem were killed.
- To escape from Herod, Joseph took Jesus and Mary to Egypt.
- Joseph returned with Mary and Jesus to Israel and settled in Nazareth, where Jesus grew up.

JESUS AT THE TEMPLE

The goal of this lesson is to look at the only event recorded regarding the childhood of Jesus.

Key Points:
- When Jesus was twelve years old, he accompanied His family to Jerusalem, where they yearly celebrated the Passover feast.
- At the end of the feast, Jesus remained behind at the temple, listening and asking questions of the teachers.
- When Joseph and Mary could not locate Jesus among their traveling companions, they returned to Jerusalem.
- After finding Jesus at the temple, being about His Father's business, the family returned to Nazareth, where Jesus was subject to them and continued to grow physically and spiritually.

JOHN BAPTIZED JESUS

The goal of this lesson is for students to see the events marking the beginning of Jesus' three years of ministry.

Key Points:
- God sent John to prepare the people for Jesus.
- John preached repentance and baptism, and under John's preaching many repented and were baptized.
- Although many wondered if John was the Messiah/Christ, John always pointed to Jesus.
- Jesus came to John to be baptized.
- As Jesus was baptized, a voice spoke from heaven and the Holy Spirit descended in the form of a dove.

New Testament Lessons

Grapevine Studies
New Testament

Lesson 2
Level 1-2

BIRTH OF JOHN

Background Bible Reading: Luke 1
Time Frame: About 400 years after Nehemiah

Zacharias and Elizabeth: *In the days of Herod the Great, Zacharias was serving as a priest in the temple in Jerusalem. Zacharias and his wife, Elizabeth, were righteous, but they had no children and were advanced in years.*

🔼 priest, righteous, walking, blameless   *Draw Zacharias and Elizabeth.*

Zacharias and the Angel: *While Zacharias was burning incense in the temple, an angel of the Lord appeared to him.* (Review where the altar of incense was in the temple.)

🔼 altar of incense   *Draw Zacharias and the angel of the Lord.*

John: *The angel told Zacharias that he and his wife would have a son, that they were to give him the name John, and that John would prepare the people for the coming of the Lord.*

🔼 make ready   *Draw Zacharias thinking about John.*

Zacharias Was Struck Mute: *Zacharias questioned the news from the angel. The angel declared that he was Gabriel and was sent by God to give Zacharias the good news. Because of his unbelief, Zacharias was struck mute by Gabriel. After Zacharias completed his priestly duties he returned home, and shortly thereafter Elizabeth conceived.*

🔼 mute   *Draw Zacharias struck mute.*

BIRTH OF JOHN

Bible Verses: Luke 1:1-80
Time Frame: About 400 years after Nehemiah

Luke 1:5-7

Luke 1:8-12

Zacharias and Elizabeth

Zacharias and the Angel

Luke 1:13-17

Luke 1:18-25

John

Zacharias Was Struck Mute

Grapevine Studies
New Testament

Lesson 2
Level 1-2

BIRTH OF JOHN

John Was Born: *Elizabeth gave birth to John, and her relatives and neighbors rejoiced with her.*

Draw baby John.

John Was Named: *On the eighth day, when the time came to name the baby, Elizabeth told those present he would be called John. When the people questioned Zacharias about the name, he wrote to confirm the choice of the name John. At once Zacharias was no longer mute and immediately began praising the Lord.*

Draw Zacharias showing a paper.

Zacharias's Prophecy: *In Zacharias's prophecy he recalled God's covenant with Abraham and David. Zacharias prophesied that John would be called "the prophet of the Most High" and prepare the way of the Lord.*

 prophesied   *Draw Zacharias prophesying.*

John Grew Up: *John grew up and was strong in spirit. He lived in the desert until the time when he was revealed to Israel.*

 strong, manifestation   *Draw John growing up.*

1. Who was king when Zacharias was a priest? *King Herod.*
2. Who appeared to Zacharias when he was in the temple? *The angel of the Lord, Gabriel.*
3. What was Zacharias told by Gabriel, and what was his response? *He and Elizabeth would have a son, but Zacharias did not believe Gabriel.*
4. What happened as a result of Zacharias's unbelief? *He was struck mute.*
5. What happened to Zacharias when John was named? *He could speak again and praised God.*
6. What do we learn about John from Zacharias's song? *John would be a prophet of the Most High and prepare the way for the Lord.*
7. What do we know about John's childhood? *He grew up strong in the Lord and lived in the desert until his manifestation to Israel.*
8. What do we learn about God from these verses? *God calls and prepares people for service to Him.*

2005

Grapevine Studies
New Testament

Lesson 2
Level 1-2

Luke 1:57-58

John Was Born

Luke 1:59-64

John Was Named

Luke 1:67-68, 76-79

Zacharias's Prophecy

Luke 1:80

John Grew Up

Lesson Review

1. Who was king when Zacharias was a priest?
2. Who appeared to Zacharias when he was in the temple?
3. What was Zacharias told by Gabriel, and what was his response?
4. What happened as a result of Zacharias's unbelief?
5. What happened to Zacharias when John was named?
6. What do we learn about John from Zacharias's song?
7. What do we know about John's childhood?
8. What do we learn about God from these verses?

Memory Verse: Luke 1:80

2005

SP 15

Grapevine Studies
Old Testament

C/E Cards
Level 3

BIRTH OF JOHN

Character/Event Cards

Create a card for the Birth of John.

- *Zacharias and his wife Elizabeth were righteous but had no children.*
- *The angel Gabriel appeared to Zacharias while he was serving as a priest in the temple and told him that he and Elizabeth would have a son.*
- *This son would prepare the people for the coming Messiah.*
- *Elizabeth and Zacharias named their son John.*
- *John grew strong in spirit and lived in the desert.*

Birth of John

Write your memory verse:

Luke 1:80

Level 2

Memory work: *There are 66 books in the Bible--39 in the Old Testament and 27 in the New Testament.*

2005

SP 16

Grapevine Studies
New Testament

Review
Level 1-2

BIRTH OF JESUS

Timeline Review

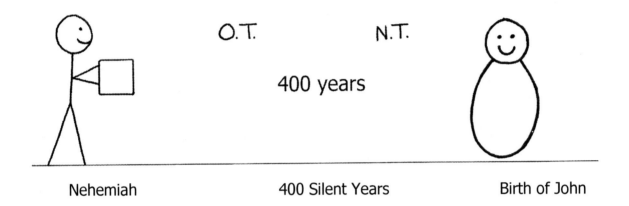

Bible Verses

Luke 1:80

2005

SP 17

Grapevine Studies
New Testament

Lesson 3
Level 1-2

BIRTH OF JESUS

Background Bible Reading: Luke 1-2; Matthew 1-2
Time Frame: Three months before the birth of John

Mary and Gabriel: *In the sixth month of Elizabeth's pregnancy, Gabriel was sent to Nazareth to Mary, a virgin, who was betrothed to Joseph. Gabriel told Mary that she would be the mother of the Son of God. Mary responded with wonder and obedience.*

 betrothed   *Draw Mary and Gabriel appearing to her.*

Mary Went to See Elizabeth: *Mary left Nazareth and went to see her relative Elizabeth. Elizabeth confirmed what the angel had told Mary, calling her "blessed among women."*

 blessed   *Draw Mary going up to embrace Elizabeth.*

Joseph and the Angel: *Before Joseph and Mary came together in marriage, Joseph discovered that Mary was pregnant. Joseph decided to divorce Mary quietly, but an angel of the Lord appeared to him, assuring him that he was to take Mary as his wife. Joseph obeyed the angel and kept Mary pure until after Jesus was born.*

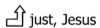 just, Jesus   *Draw Joseph in bed and the angel talking to him.*

From Nazareth to Bethlehem: *Caesar Augustus, emperor of Rome, decided that he wanted to take a census of all the earth; and as a result Joseph was required to register in Bethlehem, his family's hometown. Joseph and Mary made the trip from Nazareth to Bethlehem together.*

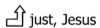 decree, census   *Draw Mary and Joseph on their way from Nazareth to Bethlehem.*

2005

Grapevine Studies
New Testament

Lesson 3
Level 1-2

BIRTH OF JESUS

Bible Verses: Luke 1:26-2:40; Matthew 1:18-2:40
Time Frame: Three months before the birth of John

Luke 1:26-31, 36-38

Luke 1:39-41, 45

Mary and Gabriel

Mary Went to See Elizabeth

Matt. 1:18-21, 24

Luke 2:1-5

Joseph and the Angel

From Nazareth to Bethlehem

SP 18

2005

Grapevine Studies
New Testament

Lesson 3
Level 1-2

BIRTH OF JESUS

Jesus Was Born: *At God's appointed time and place, among God's chosen people, the Messiah was born of woman, of the line of Abraham, and of the line of David. Jesus was wrapped in swaddling cloth and laid in a manger because of the lack of room in the inn.*

swaddling cloths   *Draw Mary and Joseph looking at baby Jesus in the manger.*

The Shepherds and the Angel: *The first people to hear about the birth of Jesus were the shepherds that were tending flocks near Bethlehem. The angel of the Lord appeared to them, telling them the wonderful news.*

Draw an angel singing before the shepherds.

The Shepherds at the Manger: *Upon receiving this great announcement, the shepherds went to see the baby for themselves. After seeing Jesus, the shepherds told all they met about the events they witnessed concerning the Christ. When others heard, they marveled at the news.*

Draw a shepherd before the manger.

1. What did the angel Gabriel tell Mary? *She would have a son, Jesus, the Son of God.*
2. How did Joseph respond to news of Mary's pregnancy? *He planned to divorce her.*
3. What did the angel tell Joseph to do, and how did he respond? *He obeyed the angel and took Mary as his wife.*
4. Why did Mary and Joseph have to travel from Nazareth to Bethlehem? *Because Caesar wanted all men to register and Joseph was required to register in Bethlehem.*
5. What happened while Joseph and Mary were in Bethlehem? *Jesus was born.*
6. Who told the shepherds that Jesus had been born? *An angel of the Lord.*
7. What did Joseph and Mary do in obedience to the Law? *They had Jesus circumcised and offered a sacrifice.*
8. What do we learn about God from these verses? *God keeps His promises and provides redemption for all men.*

2005

Grapevine Studies
New Testament

Lesson 3
Level 1-2

Luke 2:6-7

Jesus Was Born

Luke 2:8-14

The Shepherds and the Angel

Luke 2:15-20

The Shepherds at the Manger

Lesson Review

1. What did the angel Gabriel tell Mary?
2. How did Joseph respond to news of Mary's pregnancy?
3. What did the angel tell Joseph to do, and how did he respond?
4. Why did Mary and Joseph have to travel from Nazareth to Bethlehem?
5. What happened while Joseph and Mary were in Bethlehem?
6. Who told the shepherds that Jesus had been born?
7. What did Joseph and Mary do in obedience to the Law?
8. What do we learn about God from these verses?

Memory Verse: Galatians 4:4-5

2005

SP 19

Grapevine Studies
Old Testament

C/E Cards
Level 3

BIRTH OF JESUS

Character/Event Cards

Create a card for Birth of Jesus.

```
┌─────────────────────────┐
│                         │
│                         │
│      Birth of Jesus     │
│                         │
│                         │
│                         │
└─────────────────────────┘
```

Birth of Jesus

Write your memory verse:

Galatians 4:4-5

Level 2

Memory work: *The New Testament was written in the Greek language.*

2005

SP 20

Grapevine Studies　　　　　　　　　　　　　　　　　Review
New Testament　　　　　　　　　　　　　　　　　　Level 1-2

HEROD AND THE WISE MEN

Timeline Review

O.T.　　　N.T.

400 years

"400 Silent Years"　　　Birth of John　　　Birth of Jesus

Bible Verses

Galatians 4:4-5

Luke 1:80

Grapevine Studies
New Testament

Lesson 4
Level 1-2

HEROD AND THE WISE MEN

Background Bible Reading: Matthew 1-2
Time Frame: After the birth of Jesus

Herod and the Wise Men: *After the birth of Jesus, wise men went to Jerusalem, having followed a star, seeking to worship the newborn king of the Jews.*

 wise men   *Draw Herod and the wise men standing before him.*

Herod's Quest: *When Herod heard that a king had been born among the Jews, he sought to find out where the Christ would be born. Herod consulted with the chief priests and scribes to determine where the Child would be born. He was told the prophecies indicated that the Messiah would be born in Bethlehem. Herod then directed the wise men to return to him and report the child's location.*

 troubled   *Draw Herod questioning a scribe.*

The Wise Men and Jesus: *The Wise Men left Jerusalem and went to Bethlehem, where they found Jesus. They worshipped Him and presented Him with gifts. Before they left they were warned in a dream not to go to back to Herod, so they took a different route to their homes.*

star, frankincense, myrrh   *Draw the wise men before Jesus.*

2005

Grapevine Studies
New Testament

Lesson 4
Level 1-2

HEROD AND THE WISE MEN

Bible Verses: Matthew 2:1-23
Time Frame: After the birth of Jesus

Matt. 2:1-2

Matt. 2:3-8

Herod and the Wise Men

Herod's Quest

Matt. 2:9-12

The Wise Men and Jesus

2005

SP 22

Grapevine Studies
New Testament

Lesson 4
Level 1-2

HEROD AND THE WISE MEN

The Flight to Egypt: *The angel of the Lord told Joseph to take Mary and Jesus and flee to Egypt because Herod was seeking to kill Jesus.*

Draw Joseph, Mary, and Jesus fleeing to Egypt.

Herod's Rage: *Herod was furious when he saw that the wise men had disobeyed his command by not returning to him to report the whereabouts of the child. As a result, Herod ordered all male children two years old and younger living in and around Bethlehem to be killed.*

Draw Herod ordering "death."

The Return to Israel: *Herod died, and Joseph had a dream in which the angel told him to return with his family to Israel. Joseph, Mary, and Jesus returned to Israel but settled in the land of Galilee, in a town called Nazareth, instead of Bethlehem.*

Draw Joseph returning with Mary and Jesus to Nazareth.

Jesus as a Child: *In Nazareth Jesus grew up physically and grew strong spiritually.*

Draw Jesus growing up.

1. Why did the wise men travel to Jerusalem? *To worship the newborn king of the Jews.*
2. What was Herod's response to the news that a king of the Jews had been born? *He sought to locate the Child's birthplace from the chief priests, scribes and wise men.*
3. What gifts did the wise men give to Jesus? *Gold, frankincense and myrrh.*
4. Where did the angel tell Joseph to take his family and why? *To Egypt because Herod was seeking to kill Jesus.*
5. When the wise men failed to return to Herod, how did he respond? *He ordered all the children two years old and under living in and near Bethlehem to be killed.*
6. When did Joseph return with his family to Israel? *After the death of Herod.*
7. In what town did Jesus spend His childhood? *Nazareth.*
8. What do we know about Jesus as a child? *He grew up physically and became spiritually strong.*
9. What do we learn about God from these verses? *God desires and accepts the worship of all men, and like the wise men we should also seek to worship the Lord.*

2005

Grapevine Studies
New Testament

Lesson 4
Level 1-2

Matt. 2:13-15

The Flight to Egypt

Matt. 2:16-17

Herod's Rage

Matt. 2:19-23

The Return to Israel

Luke 2:40

Jesus as a Child

Lesson Review

1. Why did the wise men travel to Jerusalem?
2. What was Herod's response to the news that a king of the Jews had been born?
3. What gifts did the wise men give to Jesus?
4. Where did the angel tell Joseph to take his family and why?
5. When the wise men failed to return to Herod, how did he respond?
6. When did Joseph return with his family to Israel?
7. In what town did Jesus spend His childhood?
8. What do we know about Jesus as a child?
9. What do we learn about God from these verses?

Memory Verse: Matthew 2:11

2005

SP 23

Grapevine Studies
Old Testament

C/E Cards
Level 3

HEROD AND THE WISE MEN

Character/Event Cards

Create a card for Herod and the Wise Men.

> - *Wise men from the East followed a star that led them to find the newborn king of the Jews.*
> - *Herod wanted to find and kill the newborn king.*
> - *The wise men found Jesus, worshipped Him, and presented Him with gifts.*
> - *Herod ordered that all the male children in the Bethlehem area, age two and younger, be killed.*
> - *Joseph fled with Mary and Jesus to Egypt, where they lived until Herod died.*
> - *Jesus grew up in Nazareth, where He grew up physically and grew strong in spirit.*

Herod and the Wise Men

Write your memory verse:

Matthew 2:11

Level 2

Memory work: *The Gospels: Matthew, Mark, Luke, and John.*

2005

SP 24

Grapevine Studies
New Testament

Review
Level 1-2

JESUS AT THE TEMPLE

Timeline Review

Birth of John *Birth of Jesus* *Jesus in Egypt* Nazareth

Bible Verses

Matthew 2:11

Galatians 4:4-5

2005

SP 25

Grapevine Studies
New Testament

Lesson 5
Level 1-2

JESUS AT THE TEMPLE

Background Bible Reading: Luke 2
Time Frame: Jesus at age twelve

Passover in Jerusalem: *Following the return of Joseph, Mary, and Jesus from Egypt, Scripture records nothing more about Jesus' childhood except in Luke 2:40. As Jesus grew up, He grew strong in the Lord and was filled with wisdom and God's grace. In obedience to the Law (Ex. 23:14-17), Joseph took his family and went to Jerusalem for the celebration of the Feast of Passover.*

Passover, wisdom, grace   *Draw Joseph, Mary, and Jesus on their way to Jerusalem.*

Jesus Remained in Jerusalem: *After Passover Joseph and Mary left to go home but did not realize that Jesus had remained in Jerusalem and was not in their company.*

Draw Jesus worshipping at the temple.

Joseph and Mary Returned to Jerusalem: *When Joseph and Mary could not locate Jesus among their traveling companions and family, they returned to Jerusalem in search of their son.*

Draw Joseph and Mary returning to Jerusalem.

2005

Grapevine Studies
New Testament

Lesson 5
Level 1-2

JESUS AT THE TEMPLE

Bible Verses: Luke 2:40-51
Time Frame: Jesus at age twelve

Luke 2:40-42

Exodus 23:14-17

Passover in Jerusalem

Luke 2:43

Luke 2:44-45

Jesus Remained in Jerusalem   **Joseph and Mary Returned to Jerusalem**

2005

SP 26

Grapevine Studies
New Testament

Lesson 5
Level 1-2

JESUS AT THE TEMPLE

Jesus at the Temple: *After three days Joseph and Mary found Jesus in the temple listening to and asking questions of the teachers. The teachers were astonished at His understanding of the Law.*

 teachers   *Draw Jesus talking to a teacher.*

The Father's Business: *Upon finding Jesus, His mother questioned Him and He responded that He had remained at the temple because He had to be about His "Father's business."*

Draw Jesus talking to Mary.

Jesus Returned with His Family: *Jesus returned to Nazareth with Joseph and Mary and continued in subjection to them. He grew physically, gained wisdom, and found favor with men and in the sight of God.*

stature, favor   *Draw Jesus growing up.*

1. Why were Joseph, Mary, and Jesus going to Jerusalem? *To celebrate the Feast of Passover.*
2. Why did Joseph and Mary leave Jerusalem without Jesus? *They thought that Jesus was returning with them but traveling with some of their family or friends.*
3. What was Jesus doing at the temple? *He was listening and asking questions of the teachers.*
4. How long did it take for Joseph and Mary to find Jesus? *Three days.*
5. When Mary asked Jesus why He stayed in Jerusalem how did He respond? *He was about His Father's business.*
6. What do we know about Jesus as He grew to be man? *He was in subjection to His parents, grew up physically, gained wisdom, and found favor with men and in the sight of God.*
7. What do we learn about God from these verses? *God wants us to grow up, gain wisdom, and seek to find His favor.*

2005

Grapevine Studies
New Testament

Lesson 5
Level 1-2

Luke 2:46-47

Jesus at the Temple

Luke 2:48-50

Luke 2: 51-52

The Father's Business

Jesus Returned with His Family

Lesson Review

1. Why were Joseph, Mary, and Jesus going to Jerusalem?
2. Why did Joseph and Mary leave Jerusalem without Jesus?
3. What was Jesus doing at the temple?
4. How long did it take for Joseph and Mary to find Jesus?
5. When Mary asked Jesus why he stayed in Jerusalem how did He respond?
6. What do we know about Jesus as He grew to be a man?
7. What do we learn about God from these verses?

Memory Verse: Luke 2:52

Grapevine Studies
Old Testament

C/E Cards
Level 3

JESUS AT THE TEMPLE

Character/Event Cards

Create a card for Jesus at the Temple.

- When Jesus was twelve He traveled with His family to Jerusalem to celebrate the Passover feast.
- Jesus remained at the temple listening to and asking questions of the teachers.
- It took Joseph and Mary three days to find Jesus in Jerusalem after they discovered He was not among their family and friends returning home to Nazareth.
- Jesus was found at the temple about His Father's business.
- Jesus grew up in obedience to His parents.

Jesus at the Temple

Write your memory verse:

Luke 2:52

Level 2

Memory work: Church History: *Acts.*

2005

SP 28

Grapevine Studies
New Testament

Review
Level 1-2

JOHN BAPTIZED JESUS

Timeline Review

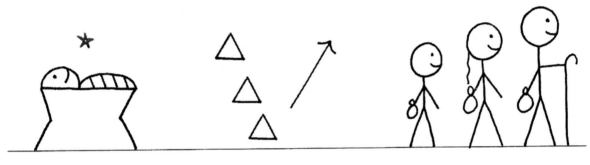

Birth of Jesus | Jesus in Egypt | Jesus at the Temple

Bible Verses

Luke 2:52

Matthew 2:11

2005

SP 29

Grapevine Studies　　　　　　　　　　　　　　　　　　　　　　　Lesson 6
New Testament　　　　　　　　　　　　　　　　　　　　　　　　Level 1-2

JOHN BAPTIZED JESUS

Background Bible Reading: Matthew 3, Luke 3
Time Frame: When Jesus was about thirty years old

John: *John grew up strong in the Lord. He wore a camel-hair cloak with a leather belt and lived in the desert. His food was wild honey and locusts.*

👆 strong　　　　　　　　　　　　　　*Draw John.*

John Preached Repentance: *At the appointed time John stepped forward and began to prepare the people for the coming of their Messiah. Being directed by God, John went into the region around the Jordan and preached repentance for the remission of sins. Many confessed their sins and were baptized.*

👆 repentance, remission, confessed　　*Draw John preaching repentance.*

John Pointed to Jesus: *When people questioned whether John was the Messiah/Christ, John pointed out that he could only baptize with water but that the One coming was mightier than he and would baptize them with the Holy Spirit and with fire.*

👆 Christ, baptize, fire　　　　　　　　*Draw John pointing to Jesus.*

John Baptized Jesus: *Jesus came to John to have John baptize him. John stated that he felt unworthy for such a task, but Jesus reminded him that it was part of God's plan. John then baptized Jesus in the Jordan River. Jesus was about thirty years old at this time, Luke 3:23.*

Draw John baptizing Jesus.

Grapevine Studies
New Testament

Lesson 6
Level 1-2

JOHN BAPTIZED JESUS

Bible Verses: Matthew 3:4-18; Luke 3:1-22
Time Frame: When Jesus was about thirty years old

Luke 1:80

Luke 3:2-6

Matt. 3:4

John

John Preached Repentance

Luke 3:15-16

Matt. 3:13-15

Luke 3:21

John Pointed to Jesus

John Baptized Jesus

2005

SP 30

Grapevine Studies
New Testament

Lesson 6
Level 1-2

JOHN BAPTIZED JESUS

Jesus and the Holy Spirit: *When Jesus came out of the water, the heavens opened and the Holy Spirit descended upon Him in the form of a dove. Then a voice spoke from heaven stating that Jesus was His beloved Son.*

 ascended   *Draw a dove descending and a voice from heaven.*

John Was Sent to Prison: *John preached to many people, including Herod the Tetrarch. John told Herod that his relationship to Herodias, his brother's wife, was sinful. For saying this John was put into prison.*

   *Draw John in chains.*

The Death of John: *Since we will not cover John later, it is important for your students to know what happened to him. Herod wanted to kill John but was afraid of the people. On Herod's birthday the opportunity arose for him to have John killed. Following John's death, his disciples buried him.*

Draw John's grave.

1. Describe John. *Strong in spirit, lived in desert, wore camel-hair clothing with leather belt, and ate wild locusts and honey.*
2. What did John preach? *Repentance.*
3. How did the people respond to John's preaching? *They confessed their sins and were baptized, but they wondered if John was the Messiah/Christ.*
4. How did John compare his baptism to how Jesus would baptize? *John baptized with water but Jesus would baptize with the Holy Spirit and fire.*
5. Who baptized Jesus? *John.*
6. What happened after Jesus was baptized? *The Holy Spirit descended upon Jesus like a dove and a voice spoke from heaven.*
7. How did John die? *Herod had him imprisoned and then beheaded.*
8. What do we learn about God from these verses? *God confirmed that Jesus is His Son and the promised Messiah.*

2005

Grapevine Studies
New Testament

Lesson 6
Level 1-2

Matt. 3:16-17

Luke 3:22

Jesus and the Holy Spirit

Luke 3:15-18, 20

Matt. 14:3-12

John Was Sent to Prison

John

The Death of John

Lesson Review

1. Describe John.
2. What did John preach?
3. How did the people respond to John's preaching?
4. How did John compare his baptism to how Jesus would baptize?
5. Who baptized Jesus?
6. What happened after Jesus was baptized?
7. How did John die?
8. What do we learn about God from these verses?

Memory Verse: Mark 1:9

2005

SP 31

Review 1

1. Who was king when Zacharias was a priest? *King Herod.*
2. Who appeared to Zacharias when he was in the temple? *The angel of the Lord, Gabriel.*
3. What was Zacharias told by Gabriel, and what was his response? *He and Elizabeth would have a son, but Zacharias did not believe Gabriel.*
4. What happened as a result of Zacharias's unbelief? *He was struck mute.*
5. What happened to Zacharias when John was named? *He could speak again and praised God.*
6. What do we learn about John from Zacharias's song? *John would be a prophet of the Most High and prepare the way for the Lord.*
7. What do we know about John's childhood? *He grew up strong in the Lord and lived in the desert until his manifestation to Israel.*
8. Recite Luke 1:80.
9. What did the angel Gabriel tell Mary? *She would have a son, Jesus, the Son of God.*
10. How did Joseph respond to news of Mary's pregnancy? *He planned to divorce her.*
11. What did the angel tell Joseph to do, and how did respond? *He obeyed the angel and took Mary as his wife.*
12. Why did Mary and Joseph have to travel from Nazareth to Bethlehem? *Because Caesar wanted all men to register and Joseph was required to register in Bethlehem.*
13. What happened while Joseph and Mary were in Bethlehem? *Jesus was born.*
14. Who told the shepherds that Jesus had been born? *An angel of the Lord.*
15. What did Joseph and Mary do in obedience to the Law? *They had Jesus circumcised, Mary completed her purification and they offered the sacrifice for purification.*
16. Recite Galatians 4:4-5.
17. Why did the wise men travel to Jerusalem? *To worship the newborn king of the Jews.*
18. What was Herod's response to the news that a king of the Jews had been born? *He sought to locate the Child's birthplace from the chief priests, scribes, and wise men.*
19. What gifts did the Wise Men give to Jesus? *Gold, frankincense and myrrh.*
20. Where did the angel tell Joseph to take his family and why? *To Egypt because Herod was seeking to kill Jesus.*

Grapevine Studies
New Testament

Review 1
Level 1-2

21. When the wise men failed to return to Herod, how did he respond? *He ordered all the children two years old and under living in and near Bethlehem to be killed.*
22. When did Joseph return with his family to Israel? *After the death of Herod.*
23. In what town did Jesus spend His childhood? *Nazareth.*
24. What do we know about Jesus as a child? *He grew up physically and became spiritually strong.*
25. Recite Matthew 2:11.
26. Why were Joseph, Mary, and Jesus going to Jerusalem? *To celebrate the Feast of Passover.*
27. Why did Joseph and Mary leave Jerusalem without Jesus? *They thought that Jesus was returning with them but traveling with some of their family or friends.*
28. What was Jesus doing at the temple? *He was listening and asking questions of the teachers.*
29. How long did it take for Joseph and Mary to find Jesus? *Three days.*
30. When Mary asked Jesus why He stayed in Jerusalem how did He respond? *He was about His Father's business.*
31. What do we know about Jesus as He grew to be a man? *He was in subjection to His parents, He grew up physically, gained wisdom, and found favor with men and in the sight of God.*
32. Recite Luke 2:52.
33. Describe John. *Strong in spirit, lived in desert, wore camel-hair clothing with leather belt, ate wild locusts and honey.*
34. What did John preach? *Repentance.*
35. How did the people respond to John's preaching? *They confessed their sins and were baptized but they wondered if John was the Messiah/Christ.*
36. How did John compare his baptism to how Jesus would baptize? *John baptized with water but Jesus would baptize with the Holy Spirit and fire.*
37. Who baptized Jesus? *John.*
38. What happened after Jesus was baptized? *The Holy Spirit descended upon Jesus like a dove and a voice spoke from heaven.*
39. How did John die? *Herod had him imprisoned and then beheaded.*
40. Recite Mark 1:9.

Level 2

41. How many books are in the New Testament? *27 books.*
42. In what language was the New Testament written? *Greek.*
43. Name the Gospel books. *Matthew, Mark, Luke and John.*

2005

SP 33

Grapevine Studies
New Testament

Section 3
Level 1-2

Section 3 Goals and Key Points

THE TEMPTATION OF JESUS

The goal of this lesson is for the students to see that Jesus was tempted in all ways, yet remained without sin, so that He is now able to help us in our time of temptation.

Key Points:
- Jesus was led into the wilderness by the Holy Spirit and fasted there for forty days.
- Satan tempted Jesus, and each time Jesus responded with Scripture: "It is written."
- Jesus was tempted throughout His earthly life yet remained without sin.
- All men are tempted, but God will not allow us to be tempted beyond what we can bear and will always provide us with a way of escape.
- Jesus helps us in our time of temptation.

SATAN

The goal of this lesson is to learn the different names and characteristics of Satan and then to study our defenses.

Key Points:
- Satan is known by many names which reveal his actions and character.
- The armor of God is given to us as a defense.
- Satan will spend eternity in the lake of fire.

THE TWELVE APOSTLES

The goal of this lesson is to learn about the twelve apostles.

Key Points:
- Jesus had many "disciples" but only twelve "apostles."
- The twelve apostles were commissioned and empowered by Jesus to preach the Gospel and heal those who were sick and demon-possessed.
- The life work of the apostles was to teach the word of God and pray.

2005

JESUS TAUGHT

The goal of this lesson is to study some of the teachings of Jesus.

Key Points:
- Jesus taught that outward sins (actions) are a result of inward sins (thoughts and motives).
- When Jesus was asked what the greatest command was, He responded by saying to love God completely and also to love your neighbor as yourself.

JESUS PRAYED

The goal of this lesson is to observe how, when, and where Jesus prayed.

Key Points:
- Jesus often prayed alone.
- Jesus prayed at different times: in the morning, after ministering all day, and before His crucifixion.
- Jesus prayed in many places: in the wilderness, on a mountain, at Gethsemane.
- Jesus taught His disciples to pray.

JESUS AND THE SEA

The goal of this lesson is to explore how Jesus demonstrated His power over the sea.

Key Points:
- Scripture records two instances where Jesus displayed His control over the wind and the sea.
- Jesus had the power to calm the wind and the sea when a tempest rose on the Sea of Galilee, threatening to capsize the boat He was riding in.
- Jesus also walked on the sea and called Peter out of the boat to do the same.

Grapevine Studies
Old Testament

C/E Cards
Level 3

JOHN BAPTIZED JESUS

Character/Event Cards

Create a card for John Baptized Jesus.

> - *John prepared the people*
> - *for the Messiah by preaching repentance and baptizing the people.*
> - *John baptized Jesus in the Jordan River.*
> - *After Jesus was baptized:*
>   1. *The Holy Spirit descended upon Jesus in the form of a dove.*
>   2. *A voice from heaven spoke confirming that Jesus was the Son of God.*
> - *John was put into prison and later beheaded.*

John Baptized Jesus

Write your memory verse:

Mark 1:9

Level 2

Memory work: *The Epistles: Romans, I & II Corinthians, Galatians.*

2005

SP 34

THE TEMPTATION OF JESUS

Timeline Review

Nazareth

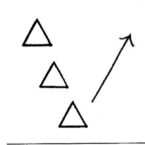

Jesus in Egypt   *Jesus at the Temple*   *John Baptized Jesus*

Bible Verses

Mark 1:9

Luke 2:52

Grapevine Studies
New Testament

Lesson 7
Level 1-2

THE TEMPTATION OF JESUS

Background Bible Reading: Matthew 4, Mark 1, Luke 4
Time Frame: When Jesus was about thirty years old

Jesus Fasted: *After being baptized and filled with the Holy Spirit, Jesus was led into the wilderness to be tempted/tested by Satan. While in the wilderness He fasted forty days and nights.*

 tempted, fasted   *Draw Jesus being led into the wilderness, and the fasting symbol.*

Stones to Bread: *Satan tempted Jesus to prove that He was the Son of God by turning stones to bread. Jesus responded by quoting Deuteronomy 8:3.*

 tempter   *Write response and scripture that he used.*

Jump Off the Temple: *Satan quoted Scripture to tempt Jesus to jump off the temple to prove that He was the Son of God. (It is interesting to note that when Satan quoted Scripture, he failed to quote all of Psalm 91:11-12.) Jesus responded by quoting Scripture.*

Write response and scripture that he used.

Worship Satan: *Satan showed Jesus all the kingdoms of the earth and their glory and said he would give Jesus all of them if Jesus would worship him. Jesus responded by quoting Scripture and then commanded Satan to leave.*

 worship   *Write response and scripture that he used.*

Grapevine Studies
New Testament

Lesson 7
Level 1-2

THE TEMPTATION OF JESUS

Bible Verses: Matthew 4:1-11; Hebrews 2:18, 4:15; I Corinthians 2:18
Time Frame: When Jesus was about thirty years old

Matt. 4:1-2

Jesus Fasted

Satan's Temptation	Jesus' Response
Matt. 4:3-4 Stones to Bread	*"It is written..."* *Deuteronomy 8:3*
Matt. 4:5-7 Jump Off the Temple	*"It is written..."* *Deuteronomy 6:16*
Matt. 4:8-10 Worship Satan	*"It is written..."* *Deuteronomy 6:13*

SP 36

2005

Grapevine Studies
New Testament

Lesson 7
Level 1-2

THE TEMPTATION OF JESUS

Jesus After the Temptation: *After Satan left, angels ministered to Jesus.*

⌂ ministered   *Draw Jesus with an angel over Him.*

Tempted but Without Sin: *Scripture tells us that Jesus was tempted in all ways, like we are, but did not sin.*

⌂ High Priest, sympathize, weakness, sin   *Draw Jesus with temptation and no sin.*

Our Temptations: *The Bible assures us that the temptations we face are common to all men. No temptation will be beyond what we can handle, and with every temptation God will provide us with a means of escape.*

⌂ temptation, tempted, escape, bear   *Draw temptation coming to man and the escape.*

Jesus and Our Temptations: *Jesus was tempted so that He could help us in our temptations.*

⌂ aid   *Draw Jesus helping us in our temptations.*

1. Where did Jesus go after He was baptized? *He was led into the wilderness to be tempted.*
2. Who tempted Jesus? *Satan.*
3. What were the three temptations of Jesus? *(1) Stones to bread, (2) throw Himself off the temple, (3) Worship Satan.*
4. How did Jesus respond to temptation? *"It is written" or with Scripture.*
5. What happened to Jesus after He was tempted? *The angels came and ministered to Him.*
6. When Jesus was tempted, did He ever sin? *NO!*
7. Will we be tempted? *Yes, but not beyond what we can bear.*
8. What does Jesus do when we are tempted? *He aids us and provides us with an escape.*
9. What do we learn about God from these verses? *God will not allow us to be tempted beyond what we can bear and will aid us when we are tempted and provide a way of escape.*

2005

Grapevine Studies
New Testament

Lesson 7
Level 1-2

Matt. 4:11

Jesus After the Temptation

Hebrews 4:15

Tempted but Without Sin

I Corinthians 10:13

Our Temptations

Hebrews 2:18

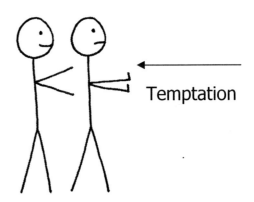

Jesus and Our Temptations

Lesson Review

1. Where did Jesus go after He was baptized?
2. Who tempted Jesus?
3. What were the three temptations of Jesus?
4. How did Jesus respond to temptation?
5. What happened to Jesus after He was tempted?
6. When Jesus was tempted, did He ever sin?
7. Will we be tempted?
8. What does Jesus do when we are tempted?
9. What do we learn about God from these verses?

Memory Verse:

Grapevine Studies
Old Testament

C/E Cards
Level 3

THE TEMPTATION OF JESUS

Character/Event Cards

Create a card for the Temptation of Jesus.

- *After Jesus was baptized the Spirit led Him into the desert where He fasted for 40 days and was tempted by Satan.*
- *Jesus responded to Satan's temptations by quoting scripture.*
- *After Jesus was tempted angels ministered to Him.*

The Temptation of Jesus

Write your memory verse:

Hebrews 4:15

Level 2

Memory work: The Epistles: Romans, I & II Corinthians, Galatians, *Ephesians, Philippians, Colossians.*

2005

SP 38

SATAN

Timeline Review

Jesus at the Temple   *John Baptized Jesus*   *Temptation of Jesus*

Bible Verses

Hebrews 4:15

Mark 1:9

Grapevine Studies
New Testament

Lesson 8
Level 1-2

SATAN

Background Bible Reading: Topical or Word Study Recommended
Time Frame: Throughout history

Serpent of Old/Deceiver: *Satan in often referred to as the Serpent of Old because of his long history of deceiving man, starting in Genesis and ending in Revelation.*

Draw Satan in the tree.

Devil or Satan: *I recommend a word study on these two names.*

⌂ Devil, Satan   *Draw Satan.*

Accuser of the Brethren: *One of the strategies of Satan is to accuse the brethren, or true believers, before God.*

⌂ accuse, brethren   *Draw Satan pointing a finger at a man.*

Angel of Light: *Another strategy of Satan is to appear as an angel of light for the purpose of deceiving men.*

⌂ light   *Draw Satan appearing as an angel of light.*

Father of Lies: *Satan is not only a liar but the father of lies, with no truth in him.*

⌂ lies, truth   *Draw Satan with lies coming out of his mouth.*

The Dragon: *Satan is also referred to as a dragon and the leader of angels (demons).*

⌂ dragon, angels   *Draw Satan as a dragon.*

2005

Grapevine Studies
New Testament

Lesson 8
Level 1-2

SATAN

Bible Verses: Various
Time Frame: Throughout history

Rev. 12:9

Serpent of Old/Deceiver

Rev. 12:9

Devil or Satan

Rev. 12:9-10

Accuser of the Brethren

II Cor. 11:14

Angel of Light

John 8:44

Father of Lies

Rev. 12:7

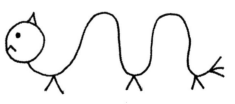

The Dragon

SP 40

2005

Grapevine Studies
New Testament

Lesson 8
Level 1-2

SATAN

Our Defense: *Begin by having your students draw a stick figure of themselves. As we cover each part of the armor, they can put that piece of armor on their stick figure.*

Be Strong in the Lord: *Before we look at our armor, we are reminded to rely upon the Lord's strength and not our own.*

- strong, stand, wiles — *Draw different things that help us stand (Bible, prayer, etc.).*

Belt of Truth: *The first piece of armor is the belt of truth. Our faith and salvation are based upon the truth of who God is and His Word.*

- truth, love — *Draw a belt on your stick figure.*

Breastplate of Righteousness: *Following truth we put on righteousness.*

- righteousness — *Draw the breastplate.*

The Gospel: *The next part of our defense is the gospel of peace.*

- gospel, peace — *Draw the shoes.*

Shield of Faith: *The shield is for extinguishing the darts thrown at us by Satan, the evil one.*

- faith, quench, fiery — *Draw the shield.*

Helmet of Salvation: *The helmet is given to us to protect our minds, for the Lord has given us a "sound mind."*

- salvation, fear, sound mind — *Draw the helmet.*

Sword of the Spirit: *The two-edged sword is given to us as weapon, and like Jesus we should use it to defeat Satan: "it is written." The sword is also an instrument that God uses to judge our thoughts and intentions.*

- powerful, discerner — *Draw the sword.*

Praying Always: *Pray always, with thanksgiving.*

- saints, thanksgiving

Satan's End: *Satan's end will be in the lake of fire, forever and ever.*

- fire, brimstone — *Draw Satan in the lake of fire.*

1. By what other names is Satan known? *See lesson.*
2. What are some of the actions of Satan? *Deceive, lie, accuse, etc.*
3. What is our defense against Satan? *Trust in the Lord, the Armor of God, and prayer.*
4. What is Satan's end? *The lake of fire, forever and ever.*
5. What do we learn about God from these verses? *God will judge Satan in the end, but until then God has given us what we need to stand against the evil one.*

2005

Grapevine Studies
New Testament

Lesson 8
Level 1-2

Our Defense

Eph. 6:10-13	Be Strong in the Lord
Eph. 6:14a	Belt of Truth
Eph. 6:14b	Breastplate of Righteousness
Eph. 6:15	The Gospel
Eph. 6:16	Shield of Faith
Eph. 6:17a	Helmet of Salvation
Eph. 6:17b	Sword of the Spirit
Eph. 6:18	Praying Always

Rev. 20:10

Satan's End

Lesson Review

1. By what other names is Satan known?
2. What are some of the actions of Satan?
3. What is our defense against Satan?
4. What is Satan's end?
5. What do we learn about God from these verses?

Memory Verse: Revelation 20:10

SP 41

2005

Grapevine Studies
Old Testament

C/E Cards
Level 3

SATAN

Character/Event Cards

Create a card for Satan.

> - *Satan is known by many names:*
>   1. *Serpent of Old*
>   2. *Deceiver*
>   3. *Devil*
>   4. *Satan*
>   5. *Accuser of the Brethren*
>   6. *Angel of light*
>   7. *Father of lies*
>   8. *Dragon*
> - *Our defense against Satan is the Word of God and the armor of God.*
> - *Satan's end will be in the lake of fire.*

Satan

Write your memory verse:

Revelation 20:10

Level 2

Memory work: The Epistles: Romans, I & II Corinthians, Galatians, Ephesians, Philippians, Colossians, *I & II Thessalonians, I & II Timothy.*

SP 42

THE TWELVE APOSTLES

Timeline Review

Jesus at the Temple   John Baptized Jesus   Temptation of Jesus

Bible Verses

Revelation 20:10

Hebrews 4:15

Grapevine Studies
New Testament

Lesson 9
Level 1-2

THE TWELVE APOSTLES

Background Bible Reading: Various Passages
Time Frame: Ministry of Jesus

Disciple: *A disciple listens, learns, and then acts upon what he has learned. (Later this term was used to describe followers of Jesus.)*

 Disciple   *Draw a teacher and a disciple listening then mimicking his actions.*

Apostle: *An apostle was an eyewitness to Jesus' life who was empowered and commissioned to be sent forth to preach the Gospel. (Later this term was used to describe believers who were prominent leaders.)*

Apostle   *Draw Jesus commissioning and sending.*

Andrew And Simon Peter: *Andrew, a disciple of John the Baptist, was with John when Jesus was pointed out to him. Realizing that Jesus was the Messiah, Andrew began following Jesus. Andrew sought out his brother, Simon Peter, to tell him about the Messiah and then brought him to Jesus.*

Draw Andrew and Simon Peter.

Philip: *Jesus called Phillip, who was from Bethsaida, to follow Him.*

Draw Philip.

Matthew: *Jesus called Matthew (Levi), the tax collector to follow Him and, he did.*

tax collector   *Draw Matthew*

James and John: *Sons of Zebedee who were fishermen and friends of Andrew and Simon.*

Draw James and John.

2005

Grapevine Studies
New Testament

Lesson 9
Level 1-2

THE TWELVE APOSTLES

Bible Verses: Various Passages
Time Frame: Ministry of Jesus

Luke 6:12-13

Disciple   Apostle

John 1:35-36, 40-42   John 1:43-44

Andrew   Simon (Peter)   Philip

Matt. 9:9-13   Matt. 10:2-4

Matthew (Levi)   James (sons of Zebedee)   John

SP 44

Grapevine Studies s
New Testament

Lesson 9
Level 1-2

THE TWELVE APOSTLES

Bartholomew (Nathaniel), Thomas, James, Lebbaeus (Thaddaeus), Simon (the Canaanite) and Judas Iscariot: *Jesus called a total of twelve of His disciples to be His apostles.*

Draw the remaining apostles.

Teacher Note: *I would also recommend a study in Church history/tradition on the lives and deaths of the apostles.*

1. What is a disciple? *One who listens and learns and then acts upon what he has learned.*
2. What is an apostle? *One who is called, commissioned, and empowered to go forth.*
3. Who were the twelve apostles of Jesus Christ? *Andrew, Simon Peter, Philip, Matthew, James, John, Bartholomew, Thomas, James, Lebbaeus, Simon, Judas Iscariot.*
4. What do we learn about God from these verses? *God desires first that we become His disciple and then go and make other disciples.*

2005

Grapevine Studies
New Testament

Lesson 9
Level 1-2

Mark 3:16-19

Bartholomew

Thomas

James
(son of Alphaeus)

Lebbaeus

Simon
(the Canaanite)

Judas Iscariot

Lesson Review

1. What is a disciple?
2. What is an apostle?
3. Who were the twelve apostles of Jesus Christ?
4. What do we learn about God from these verses?

Memory Verse: Matthew 28:19-20

2005

SP 45

Grapevine Studies
Old Testament

C/E Cards
Level 3

THE TWELVE APOSTLES

Character/Event Cards

Create a card for the Twelve Apostles.

> - *A disciple is one who listens, learns and then acts upon what he has learned.*
> - *Jesus had Twelve Apostles: Andrew, Simon Peter, Philip, Matthew, James, John, Bartholomew, Thomas, James, Lebbaeus, Simon, Judas Iscariot.*

The Twelve Apostles

Write your memory verse:

Matthew 28:19-20

Level 2

Memory work: The Epistles: Romans, I & II Corinthians, Galatians, Ephesians, Philippians, Colossians, I & II Thessalonians, I & II Timothy, *Titus, Philemon, Hebrews.*

2005

SP 46

Grapevine Studies
New Testament

Review
Level 1-2

JESUS TAUGHT

Timeline Review

John Baptized Jesus   Temptation of Jesus   Twelve Apostles

Bible Verses

Matthew 28:19-20

Revelation 20:10

2005

SP 47

Grapevine Studies
New Testament

Lesson 10
Level 1-2

JESUS TAUGHT

Background Bible Reading: Matthew 5-6, 22
Time Frame: Ministry of Jesus

Murder and Anger: *As Jesus instructed His disciples, He often referred to what they had been taught in the Law (New Testament). The disciples knew what the Law taught about murder, but Jesus elaborated by addressing the inward issue of anger and expressions of anger.*

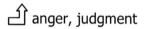 anger, judgment   *Draw a man angry at another man.*

Yes and No: *Jesus taught His disciples not to swear an oath by anything on earth or in heaven but instead let their "yes" be yes and their "no" be no.*

swear   *Draw a woman saying "Yes" and a man saying "No."*

Love Your Enemies: *In place of hate and the actions associated with someone being our "enemy," Jesus taught that His disciples were to love, bless, do good to, and pray for their enemies.*

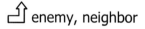 enemy, neighbor   *Draw a man praying and blessing his enemy.*

Charitable Deeds: *When we do charitable deeds it should be for the Lord, and the only reward we should seek should be from Him.*

charitable   *Draw a man giving another man a drink with God watching.*

2005

Grapevine Studies
New Testament

Lesson 10
Level 1-2

JESUS TAUGHT

Bible Verses: Matthew 5:21-45; 6:1-34; 22:36-40
Time Frame: Ministry of Jesus

Matt. 5:21-22

Murder and Anger

Matt. 5:33-34, 37

Yes and No

Matt. 5:43-45

Love Your Enemies

Matt. 6:1-2

Charitable Deeds

SP 48

2005

Grapevine Studies
New Testament

Lesson 10
Level 1-2

JESUS TAUGHT

Two Masters: *We all must chose who we will serve in our life: God or money.*

 mammon   *Draw the symbols for God and money.*

Do Not Worry: *God reminds us not to worry because He is able to provide for our every need. God demonstrates His provision throughout Creation.*

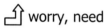 worry, need   *Draw a man looking at flowers with birds above.*

The Greatest Commandment: *When Jesus was asked "What is the greatest commandment," He responded by saying love God completely and also love your neighbor as yourself.*

 testing, love   *Draw a man loving God and a man loving others.*

1. To what can anger lead? *Speaking evil against others, hate, and murder.*
2. What did Jesus teach about swearing? *We are not to swear but let our "yes" mean yes and our "no" mean no.*
3. How are we to treat our enemies? *We are to love, bless, do good to, and pray for our enemies.*
4. When we do charitable deeds, from whom should we seek recognition? *God alone.*
5. What two masters can we serve? *God or mammon.*
6. When we worry, what are we to remember? *Creation and that God will take care of our needs.*
7. What is the greatest commandment? *Love God totally.*
8. What is the second greatest commandment? *Love our neighbor like we love ourselves.*
9. What do we learn about God from these verses? *God is concerned not only with our outward actions but also with our inward thoughts and attitudes.*

2005

Grapevine Studies
New Testament

Lesson 10
Level 1-2

Matt. 6:24

Matt. 6:25, 33-34

Two Masters

Do Not Worry

Matt. 22:36-40

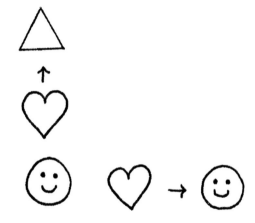

The Greatest Commandment

Lesson Review

1. To what can anger lead?
2. What did Jesus teach about swearing?
3. How are we to treat our enemies?
4. When we do charitable deeds, from whom should we seek recognition?
5. What two masters can we serve?
6. When we worry, what are we to remember?
7. What is the greatest commandment?
8. What is the second greatest commandment?
9. What do we learn about God from these verses?

Memory Verse: Matthew 22:37-39

2005

SP 49

Grapevine Studies
Old Testament

C/E Cards
Level 3

JESUS TAUGHT

Character/Event Cards

Create a card for Jesus Taught.

- *Jesus taught*
  1. *The greatest commandment is to love God first and then love others.*
  2. *Our thoughts and attitudes will show in our actions.*
  3. *Do not swear.*
  4. *Love your enemies*
  5. *Charitable deeds should be done for God to see and not for reward.*
  6. *No man can serve God and money.*
  7. *Do not worry.*

Jesus Taught

Write your memory verse:

Matthew 22:37-39

Level 2

Memory work: The Epistles: Romans, I & II Corinthians, Galatians, Ephesians, Philippians, Colossians, I & II Thessalonians, I & II Timothy, Titus, Philemon, Hebrews, *James, I & II Peter.*

2005

SP 50

Grapevine Studies
New Testament

Review
Level 1-2

JESUS PRAYED

Timeline Review

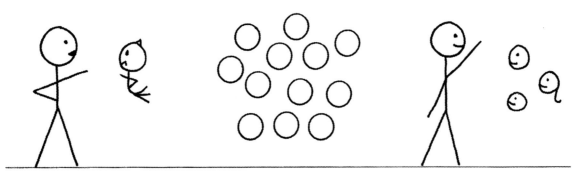

Temptation of Jesus Twelve Apostles Jesus Taught

Bible Verses

Matthew 22:37-39

Matthew 28:19-20

2005

SP 51

Grapevine Studies
New Testament

Lesson 11
Level 1-2

JESUS PRAYED

Background Bible Reading: Various
Time Frame: Ministry of Jesus

Jesus Prayed: *Jesus set an example for us in prayer: He prayed often, alone, and for God's will to be done. In these verses we see some examples of when and where Jesus prayed.*

prayed, solitary

Fill in the blanks.

Grapevine Studies
New Testament

Lesson 11
Level 1-2

JESUS PRAYED

Bible Verses: Various
Time Frame: Ministry of Jesus

Jesus Prayed

	When	Where
Matt. 14:23	After sending the multitudes away, in the evening	Mountain
Mark 1:35	Early in the morning	Solitary place
Luke 5:15-16	After teaching and healing	Wilderness
Luke 6:12	All night	Mountain
Mark 14:32-36	Before His trial and crucifixion	Gethsemane

2005

SP 52

Grapevine Studies
New Testament

Lesson 11
Level 1-2

JESUS PRAYED

When You Pray: *Jesus wanted His disciples to see prayer differently than they had before. He wanted them to understand that prayer did not need to be public and with many repetitive words and phrases but rather a private encounter with the Lord of Heaven.*

📖 hypocrites, secret, vain repetitions, heathen

Jesus Taught His Disciples to Pray: *I recommend your own personal study of, the words used in this prayer, cross-referencing it with Luke 11:2-4.*

📖 hallowed, kingdom   *See notes on page opposing page.*

1. When did Jesus pray? *In the morning, at night, and after He had taught and healed.*
2. Where did Jesus pray? *On mountains and in solitary places.*
3. What are we to do when we pray? *Pray in secret, remembering God knows our needs.*
4. What are we not to do when we pray? *Pray to be seen by others and use vain repetitions and many words.*
5. What do we learn about God from these verses? *God wants us to pray using Jesus as an example.*

2005

Grapevine Studies
New Testament

Lesson 11
Level 1-2

| Matt. 6:5-8 |

When You Pray

Do	Do Not
Pray in a secret place	Pray to be seen by others
Remember your Father knows your needs	Use vain repetitions or many words

| Matt. 6:9-13 |

Jesus Taught His Disciples to Pray

_____
_____
_____
_____
_____
_____
_____
_____
_____
_____

Note: For young writers you may want to have them stick figure one or two parts of this prayer.

Lesson Review

1. When did Jesus pray?
2. Where did Jesus pray?
3. What are we to do when we pray?
4. What are we not to do when we pray?
5. What do we learn about God from these verses?

Memory Verse: Mark 1:35

Grapevine Studies
Old Testament

C/E Cards
Level 3

JESUS PRAYED

Character/Event Cards

Create a card for Jesus Prayed.

> - *Jesus gave us an example in prayer.*
>   1. *He prayed in the morning, evening and after He had ministered.*
>   2. *He prayed on mountains and in solitary places.*
>   3. *He prayed often.*
> - *Jesus taught His disciples to pray.*

Jesus Prayed

Write your memory verse:

Mark 1:35

Level 2

Memory work: The Epistles: Romans, I & II Corinthians, Galatians, Ephesians, Philippians, Colossians, I & II Thessalonians, I & II Timothy, Titus, Philemon, Hebrews, James, I & II Peter, *I, II & III John, Jude.*

2005

SP 54

JESUS AND THE SEA

Timeline Review

Twelve Apostles   Jesus Taught   Jesus Prayed

Bible Verses

Mark 1:35

Matthew 22:37-39

Grapevine Studies
New Testament

Lesson 12
Level 1-2

JESUS AND THE SEA

Background Bible Reading: Matthew 8, 14
Time Frame: Ministry of Jesus

Jesus and His Disciples: *In the following passages we will see that Jesus had power over Creation. When He spoke, Creation responded. One evening, after a day of ministry, Jesus and His disciples got into a boat and set out on the Sea of Galilee.*

Draw calm waters and the boat.

A Great Tempest Arose: *After they set out on the sea, a great tempest suddenly came upon them. The waves threatened to overtake them, but Jesus slept in spite of the storm.*

 tempest
Draw the boat on stormy seas.

The Disciples Cried Out: *The disciples, fearing that the boat would capsize, woke Jesus and cried out for Him to save them.*

Draw the disciples around Jesus.

Jesus Calmed the Storm: *Jesus arose and spoke to the wind and the sea. Immediately the winds stopped and the sea became calm. The disciples marveled that the winds and the sea obeyed Him.*

Draw the boat on calm seas.

2005

Grapevine Studies
New Testament

Lesson 12
Level 1-2

JESUS AND THE SEA

Bible Verses: Matthew 8:23-27, 14:22-33
Time Frame: Ministry of Jesus

Matt. 8:23

Jesus and His Disciples

Matt. 8:24

A Great Tempest Arose

Matt. 8:25

The Disciples Cried Out

Matt. 8:26-27

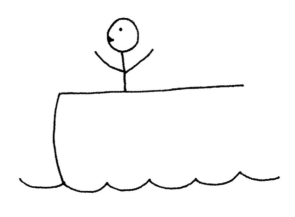

Jesus Calmed the Sea

2005

SP 56

Grapevine Studies
New Testament

Lesson 12
Level 1-2

JESUS AND THE SEA

Jesus Prayed: *Jesus often went alone upon a mountain to pray, even after a long day of ministry.*

Draw Jesus on a mountain praying and a boat sailing.

Jesus Walked on Water: *On one occasion, Jesus sent the disciples out across the Sea of Galilee in their boat. Jesus came to them walking on the water, which caused great fear among the disciples.*

 watch

Draw Jesus walking on the sea towards a boat.

Jesus Calmed the Disciples: *Jesus spoke to the disciples to let them know that it was Him and not a ghost.*

Draw Jesus talking to the disciples.

Peter Walked on Water: *Peter asked Jesus to command him to come to Him on the water. When Peter got out of the boat, he looked at the waves, became afraid, and began to sink. Jesus seized Peter by the hand and asked him why he doubted. When the disciples saw these things happen, they proclaimed Jesus to be the Son of God.*

 worshipped

Draw Peter slightly in the water with Jesus holding his hand.

1. What was Jesus doing when the tempest arose? *He was sleeping.*
2. How did Jesus calm the sea? *He spoke to the wind and the waves, and it was so.*
3. How did the disciples respond when Jesus calmed the sea? *They marveled.*
4. How did the disciples respond when they saw Jesus walking on the water? *They thought He was a ghost.*
5. Who got out of the boat to walk on the water with Jesus? *Peter.*
6. What did the disciples do when Jesus and Peter walked on the water? *They worshipped Him and proclaimed Him to be the Son of God.*
7. What do we learn about God from these verses? *God has control over all of Creation, and nothing that happens to us is out of His control.*

2005

Grapevine Studies
New Testament

Lesson 12
Level 1-2

Matt. 14:22-23

Matt. 14:24-25

Jesus Prayed

Jesus Walked on Water

Matt. 14:26-27

Matt. 14:28-33

Jesus Calmed the Disciples

Peter Walked on Water

Lesson Review

1. What was Jesus doing when the tempest arose?
2. How did Jesus calm the sea?
3. How did the disciples respond when Jesus calmed the sea?
4. How did the disciples respond when they saw Jesus walking on the water?
5. Who got out of the boat to walk on the water with Jesus?
6. What did the disciples do when Jesus and Peter walked on the water?
7. What do we learn about God from these verses?

Memory Verse: Matthew 8:27

2005

SP 57

Review 2

1. Where did Jesus go after He was baptized? *He was lead into the wilderness to be tempted.*
2. Who tempted Jesus? *Satan.*
3. What were the three temptations of Jesus? *1) stone to bread 2) throw Himself off the temple 3) Worship Satan.*
4. How did Jesus respond to temptation? *"It is written" or with scripture.*
5. What happened to Jesus after He was tempted? *The angels came and ministered to Him.*
6. When Jesus was tempted did He ever sin? *NO!*
7. Will we be tempted? *Yes, but not beyond what we can bear.*
8. What does Jesus do when we are tempted? *He aids us and provides us with an escape.*
9. Recite Hebrews 4:15.
10. By what other names is Satan known? *See lesson.*
11. What are some of the actions of Satan? *Deceive, lie, accuse, etc.*
12. What is our defense against Satan? *Trust in the Lord, the Armor of God, prayer.*
13. What is Satan's end? *The Lake of Fire, forever and ever.*
14. Recite Revelation 20:10.
15. What is a disciple? *One who listens and learns and then acts upon what he has learned.*
16. What is an apostle? *One who is called, commissioned and empowered to go forth.*
17. Who were the Twelve Apostles of Jesus Christ? *Andrew, Simon Peter, Philip, Matthew, James, John, Bartholomew, Thomas, James, Lebbaeus, Simon, Judas Iscariot.*
18. What did Jesus empower His apostles to accomplish? *Cast out unclean spirits/demons and heal the sick.*
19. What commission did Jesus His apostles? *Go and make disciples.*
20. Name three things the apostles did as their life work. *They made disciples, prayed and taught the Word.*

Grapevine Studies
New Testament
Review 2
Level 1-2

21. Recite Matthew 28:19-20.
22. To what can anger lead? *Speaking evil against others, hate, and murder.*
23. What did Jesus teach about swearing? *We are not to swear but let our "yes" mean yes and our "no' mean no.*
24. How are we to treat our enemies? *We are to love, bless, do good and pray for our enemies.*
25. When we do charitable deeds, from whom should we seek recognition? *God alone.*
26. What two masters can we serve? *God or mammon.*
27. When we worry, what are we to remember? *Creation and that God will take care of our needs.*
28. What is the greatest commandment? *Love God totally.*
29. What is the second greatest commandment? *Love our neighbor like we love ourselves.*
30. Recite Matthew 22:37-39.
31. When did Jesus pray? *In the morning, at night and after He had taught and healed.*
32. Where did Jesus pray? *On mountains and in solitary places.*
33. What are we to do when we pray? *Pray in secret remembering God knows our needs.*
34. What are we not to do when we pray? *Pray to be seen by others and use vain repetitions and many words.*
35. Recite Mark 1:35.
36. What was Jesus doing when the tempest arose? *He was sleeping.*
37. How did Jesus calm the sea? *By speaking to the wind and the waves and it was so.*
38. How did the disciple's respond when Jesus calmed the sea? *They marveled.*
39. How did the disciples respond when they saw Jesus walking on the water? *They thought He was a ghost.*
40. Who got out of the boat to walk on the water with Jesus? *Peter.*
41. What did the disciples do when Jesus and Peter walked on the water? *They worshipped Him and proclaimed Him to be the Son of God.*
42. Recite Matthew 8:27.

Level 2

43. Name the books of the New Testament. *Matthew, Mark, Luke John, Acts, Romans, I & II Corinthians, Galatians, Ephesians, Philippians, Colossians, I & II Thessalonians, I & II Timothy, Titus, Philemon, Hebrews, James, I & II Peter, I, II & III John, Jude and Revelation.*

SP 59

Section 4 Goals and Key Points

JESUS FED THE MULTITUDES

The goal of this lesson is to understand how Jesus cared for the spiritual condition and physical needs of people.

Key Points:
- On two separate occasions Jesus multiplied little to feed many.
    1. With five loaves and two fish Jesus fed 5,000.
    2. With seven loaves and a few small fish Jesus fed 7,000.
- Each time Jesus fed the multitudes there were baskets of leftovers.

JESUS HEALED THE SICK

The goal of this lesson is to see to how Jesus cared for those who were sick and lame.

Key Points:
- Throughout Jesus' ministry He healed the sick, deaf, mute, blind, lame, and diseased.
- Often the sick and lame were brought by others to Jesus to be healed.
- Many of those who were healed praised God and gave thanks to Jesus.
- People who saw the healings were amazed and praised God.

JESUS HEALED THE DEMON-POSSESSED

The goal of this lesson is to show how Jesus cared for those who were demon-possessed.

Key Points:
- Demons or unclean spirits possessed many people in Jesus' day.
- Often those who were demon-possessed came to Jesus, and He delivered and healed them.
- Jesus gave His disciples authority to cast out demons.
- Scripture warns that only believers have the authority to cast out demons in Jesus' name.

JESUS RAISED THE DEAD

The goal of this lesson is to establish the fact that Jesus raised people from the dead.

Key Points:
- Scripture records that Jesus raised people from the dead, including the widow's son and Jairus' daughter.
- Jesus also raised Lazarus from the dead after he had been in the tomb four days.
- When Jesus raised Lazarus from the dead, many Jews believed.

JESUS ENTERED JERUSALEM

The goal of this lesson is to examine the events surrounding the last few days of Jesus' earthly life, beginning with His triumphal entry into Jerusalem.

Key Points:
- After Jesus raised Lazarus from the dead, the chief priests began plotting how to kill both Jesus and Lazarus, because the people believed in Jesus.
- Jesus entered Jerusalem riding on a colt while the people greeted Him by spreading their cloaks on the road, singing, and waving leafy branches before Him.
- After entering Jerusalem, Jesus went to the temple area and chased out the money changers.
- Jesus also taught and healed people while in Jerusalem in the days preceding the Feast of Passover.

THE LAST SUPPER

The goal of this lesson is to understand the events that occurred as Jesus and the disciples celebrated the Last Supper.

Key Points:
- Jesus told His disciples about His coming death.
- Jesus celebrated the Last Supper with His disciples.
- Judas betrayed Jesus to the chief priest.
- Jesus warned His disciples that they would all stumble.

Grapevine Studies
Old Testament

C/E Cards
Level 3

JESUS AND THE SEA

Character/Event Cards

Create a card for Jesus and the Sea.

> On two separate occasions Jesus interacted with the sea.
> 1. Jesus showed that He had power over the wind and sea by commanding them to be at peace and they were.
> 2. Jesus demonstrated His power over the sea by walking on water and having Peter do the same.
>
> As a result of Jesus showing His power over the sea the Disciples marveled and worshipped Him.

Jesus and the Sea

Write your memory verse:

Matthew 8:27

Level 2

Memory work: The Epistles: Romans, I & II Corinthians, Galatians, Ephesians, Philippians, Colossians, I & II Thessalonians, I & II Timothy, Titus, Philemon, Hebrews, James, I & II Peter, I, II & III John, Jude, and Revelation.

2005

SP 60

Grapevine Studies　　　　　　　　　　　　　　　　　　　　　　　Review
New Testament　　　　　　　　　　　　　　　　　　　　　　　　Level 1-2

JESUS FED THE MULTITUDES

Timeline Review

Jesus Taught　　　　　Jesus Prayed　　　　　Jesus and the Sea

Bible Verses

Matthew 8:27

Mark 1:35

Grapevine Studies
New Testament

Lesson 13
Level 1-2

JESUS FED THE MULTITUDES

Background Bible Reading: Mark 8; Luke 9
Time Frame: Ministry of Jesus

Jesus and the Crowd: *Jesus and His disciples departed to a private place near Bethsaida, but when news spread of their whereabouts, a crowd gathered to hear Him. Jesus taught the people about the kingdom of God and healed many.*

🏠 kingdom of God

Draw Jesus talking to the crowd.

Fives Loaves and Two Fish: *As evening approached, the twelve disciples spoke to Jesus about sending the people away for the night. Jesus desired to feed the people before sending them away, but the only food available was two fish and five loaves.*

Draw Jesus with loaves and fish.

Jesus Fed 5,000: *Jesus took the loaves and fish, blessed them, and gave them to the disciples to distribute among the 5,000 men (plus women and children).*

Draw people eating the bread.

Twelve Baskets of Leftovers: *When the people had eaten their fill, the disciples picked up twelve baskets full of leftovers.*

Draw a disciple with twelve baskets of leftovers.

Grapevine Studies
New Testament

Lesson 13
Level 1-2

JESUS FED THE MULTITUDES

Bible Verses: Luke 9:10-17; Mark 8:1-9
Time Frame: Ministry of Jesus

Luke 9:10-11

Jesus and the Crowd

Luke 9:12-13

Fives Loaves and Two Fish

Luke 9:14-16

Jesus Fed 5,000

2005

Luke 9:17

Twelve Baskets of Leftovers

SP 62

Grapevine Studies
New Testament

Lesson 13
Level 1-2

JESUS FED THE MULTITUDES

Jesus and the Crowd: *Word of Jesus had spread throughout the area. A crowd had been gathered for three days listening to Him. When Jesus looked upon them, He had compassion on them and desired to feed them. Being in the wilderness, the disciples asked how they could feed such a large crowd.*

Draw Jesus teaching the crowd.

Seven Loaves: *Jesus asked His disciples what food they had and they told Him seven loaves of bread and a few small fish.*

Draw Jesus with a loaf and a small fish.

Jesus Fed 4,000: *Jesus took the loaves and fish, and after giving thanks He gave them to His Disciples to distribute to the crowd.*

Draw people eating.

Seven Baskets of Leftovers: *When the people had eaten their fill, the disciples picked up seven large baskets full of leftovers. After the crowd had eaten, Jesus sent them home.*

Draw a disciple with seven baskets of leftovers.

1. When Jesus asked the disciple, to feed the crowds how did they respond? *By telling Jesus that they didn't have enough food to feed the crowds.*
2. What did Jesus do with the fish and loaves? *He gave thanks and blessed the loaves and fish.*
3. How many people did Jesus feed with five loaves and two fish? *5,000 men.*
4. How many people did Jesus feed with seven loaves and a few small fish? *4,000 men.*
5. What do we learn about God from these verses? *God is not only concerned about our spiritual well-being but also about our physical needs. God is able to provide for our physical needs.*

2005

Grapevine Studies
New Testament

Lesson 13
Level 1-2

Mark 8:1-4

Mark 8:5

Jesus and the Crowd

Seven Loaves

Mark 8:6-7

Mark 8:8-9

Jesus Fed 4,000

Seven Baskets of Leftovers

Lesson Review

1. When Jesus asked the disciple, to feed the crowds, how did they respond?
2. What did Jesus do with the fish and loaves?
3. How many people did Jesus feed with five loaves and two fish?
4. How many people did Jesus feed with seven loaves and a few small fish?
5. What do we learn about God from these verses?

Memory Verse: Luke 9:16

2005

SP 63

Grapevine Studies
Old Testament

C/E Cards
Level 3

JESUS FED THE MULTITUDES

Character/Event Cards

Create a card for Jesus Fed the Multitudes.

> On two separate occasions Jesus fed multitudes of people.
>
> 1. Jesus fed 5,000 men with five loaves of bread and two fish. Twelve baskets of leftovers were picked up.
>
> 2. Jesus fed 7,000 men with seven loaves and a few small fish. Seven baskets of leftovers were picked up.
>
> Jesus cared not only for the spiritual needs of people, but also their physical needs.

Jesus Fed the Multitudes

Write your memory verse:

Luke 9:16

Level 2

Memory work: *The Twelve Apostles: Andrew, Simon (Peter), Phillip.*

SP 64

JESUS HEALED THE SICK

Timeline Review

Jesus Prayed

Jesus and the Sea

Fed the Multitudes

Bible Verses

Luke 9:16

Matthew 8:27

Grapevine Studies
New Testament

Lesson 14
Level 1-2

JESUS HEALED THE SICK

Background Bible Reading: Mark 2, 7, 10; Luke 17
Time Frame: Ministry of Jesus

Jesus in Galilee: *While Jesus was proclaiming the gospel in Galilee, people from the surrounding area came to hear Him and to be healed of various sicknesses and diseases.*

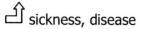 sickness, disease   *Draw Jesus and a healed man jumping for joy.*

The Sick in Gennesaret: *When the people of the area of Gennesaret heard that Jesus had come to their area, they ran and brought the sick to Him and He healed them.*

 sick, hem of His garment, well   *Draw Jesus healing.*

The Paralytic and the Roof: *While Jesus was in a home in Capernaum, He preached the Word to the people. Four men carried their friend, a paralytic, on a mat to the house so that Jesus could heal the man. Because of the large crowd, the men could not get their friend to Jesus, so they made a hole in the roof and lowered the paralytic man through the roof to where Jesus was teaching.*

paralytic   *Draw a man being lowered through the roof to Jesus.*

The Paralytic Healed: *Jesus forgave the paralytic of his sins and then healed him. This caused consternation in the minds of the scribes who were present. Jesus wanted them to understand that He was indeed the Son of Man and had authority to heal and to forgive sins. The people were amazed, and the paralytic arose from his mat and glorified God.*

scribes, Son of Man   *Draw Jesus and the healed paralytic with his mat.*

2005

Grapevine Studies
New Testament

Lesson 14
Level 1-2

JESUS HEALED THE SICK

Bible Verses: Various
Time Frame: Ministry of Jesus

Matt. 4:23

Jesus in Galilee

Mark 6:53-56

The Sick in Gennesaret

Mark 2:1-5

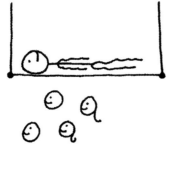

The Paralytic and the Roof

Mark 2:11-12

The Paralytic Healed

2005

SP 66

Grapevine Studies
New Testament

Lesson 14
Level 1-2

JESUS HEALED THE SICK

The Deaf and Mute: *A deaf and mute man was brought to Jesus, and Jesus took him aside and healed him.*

 deaf, impediment   *Draw Jesus and a deaf and mute boy speaking and hearing.*

The Blind Beggar: *As Jesus and his disciples traveled out of Jericho, they passed Bartimaeus, a blind beggar. As Jesus neared, Bartimaeus called out to Jesus from among the crowd. Jesus called Bartimaeus to Himself and then healed him of his blindness.*

Draw Bartimaeus being healed.

The Ten Lepers: *As Jesus traveled to Jerusalem, He passed through a village which had ten lepers living nearby. The lepers cried out to Jesus, and Jesus told them to go and show themselves to the priest (Leviticus 13-14). As the lepers were on their way to see the priest they were healed.*

 leper   *Draw a leper crying out to Jesus.*

The Leper Gave Thanks: *Only one of the ten lepers, a Samaritan, returned to give thanks and worship Jesus.*

 Samaritan   *Draw one leper bowing down at Jesus' feet.*

1. What kinds of sicknesses and ailments did Jesus heal? *The deaf, mute, blind, lepers and the paralytics.*
2. Where did Jesus heal? *In various cities, on the roadways, and in homes.*
3. What was the response of some of those who were healed? *They thanked Jesus and worshipped and praised God.*
4. How did the scribes respond to Jesus healing people and forgiving them of their sins? *They questioned Jesus' authority to forgive sins.*
5. What do we learn about God from these verses? *God can heal those who are sick with any sickness, disease, or ailment.*

2005

Grapevine Studies
New Testament

Lesson 14
Level 1-2

Mark 7:31-35

The Deaf and Mute

Mark 10:46-52

The Blind Beggar

Luke 17:11-14

The Ten Lepers

Luke 17:15-16

The Leper Gave Thanks

Lesson Review

1. What kinds of sicknesses and ailments did Jesus heal?
2. Where did Jesus heal?
3. What was the response of some of those who were healed?
4. How did the scribes respond to Jesus healing people and forgiving them of their sins?
5. What do we learn about God from these verses?

Memory Verse: Matthew 4:23

2005

SP 67

Grapevine Studies
Old Testament

C/E Cards
Level 3

JESUS HEALED THE SICK

Character/Event Cards

Create a card for Jesus Healed the Sick.

> - *Jesus healed many kinds of sicknesses and diseases, those who were:*
>   1. *Deaf*
>   2. *Blind*
>   3. *Mute*
>   4. *Palsy*
>   5. *Lepers*
>
> - *Many of those who were healed worshipped and thanked Jesus for healing them.*
> - *Jesus also forgave the sick of their sins.*

Jesus Healed the Sick

Write your memory verse:

Matthew 4:23

Level 2

Memory work: The Twelve Apostles: Andrew, Simon (Peter), Phillip, *Matthew (Levi), James, John.*

2005

SP 68

Grapevine Studies
New Testament

Review
Level 1-2

JESUS HEALED THE DEMON-POSSESSED

Timeline Review

Jesus and the Sea *Jesus Fed the Multitudes* *Jesus Healed the Sick*

Bible Verses

Matthew 4:23

Luke 9:16

2005

SP 69

Grapevine Studies
New Testament

Lesson 15
Level 1-2

JESUS HEALED THE DEMON-POSSESSED

Background Bible Reading: Mark 1, 5; Luke 4, 9-10; Acts 19
Time Frame: Ministry of Jesus

Demon: *An evil spirit who seeks the worship of men and tries to draw men away from the worship of the one true God.*

 demon   *Draw a man bowing down to a demon.*

Unclean Spirit: *An evil spirit who entices men to do evil and opposes God.*

 unclean spirit   *Draw a demon behind a man enticing him towards "evil."*

Jesus Healed the Sick and Demon-Possessed: *There are many passages that speak of Jesus casting out demons. Jesus often healed people who came to Him, whether they had a sickness/disease or were demon-possessed. Jesus demonstrated His authority over demons throughout His earthly ministry.*

demon possessed   *Draw Jesus healing people and casting out demons.*

2005

Grapevine Studies
New Testament

Lesson 15
Level 1-2

JESUS HEALED THE DEMON-POSSESSED

Bible Verses: Various
Time Frame: Ministry of Jesus

Demon: *A god or evil spirit who seeks men who will worship it instead of the one true God.**

Unclean spirit: *An evil spirit, entices men to do evil, opposes God.**

| Mark 1:32-34 | Luke 4:40-41 |

Jesus Healed the Sick and Demon Possessed

* These definitions are taken from *The Complete Word Study New Testament*, AMG Publishers, edited by Spiros Zodihiates, Th.D.

2005

SP 70

Grapevine Studies
New Testament

Lesson 15
Level 1-2

JESUS HEALED THE DEMON-POSSESSED

Man in the Synagogue: *When Jesus came to Capernaum, He taught in the synagogue, and the people were amazed at the authority with which He taught. A man at the synagogue had an unclean spirit and cried out, acknowledging that Jesus was the "Holy One of God." Jesus rebuked the evil spirit and then cast it out of the man. Those who saw this were also amazed at the power Jesus had over unclean spirits.*

☝ synagogue, amazed   *Draw the demon saying "the Holy One of God."*

Man in the Tombs: *Upon arriving in the country of the Gadarenes, Jesus was confronted by a man who was demon-possessed. This unclean spirit knew who Jesus was: "Son of the Most High God." After Jesus cast out the demon, the people were amazed to find the man dressed and in his right mind. The man desired to follow Jesus, but Jesus instructed him to remain and tell others what the Lord had done for him.*

☝ right mind, afraid   *Draw Jesus casting out a demon of a man.*

Disciples and Demons: *When Jesus sent-out the seventy disciples, He commanded them to preach the kingdom of God and to heal the sick and demon-possessed. When the seventy returned, they reported to Jesus all they had done. Jesus warned them not to focus on the fact that they had authority over demons but rather that their names were recorded in heaven.*

☝ thy name, power   *Draw a book.*

Warning: *Paul cast out demons in the name of Jesus. Seven sons of a Jewish high priest tried to exorcise a demon by imitating Paul's method of using Jesus' name. The demon told these men that it knew Jesus and Paul but it did not know them. The demon then attacked the men and publicly humiliated them. This caused fear in the city of Ephesus, where God's Word was proclaimed and obeyed.*

☝ exorcise, know   *Draw a demon and men running away.*

1. What is a demon? *A spirit who seeks men who will worship it instead of the one true God.*
2. What is an unclean spirit? *An evil spirit who entices men to do evil and is opposed to God.*
3. What did Jesus do when He encountered people who were possessed with an evil spirit? *He rebuked and then cast out the demon/evil spirit.*
4. What did the demons/unclean spirits say about Jesus? *They called Him the Holy One of God and The Son of the Most High God.*
5. To whom did Jesus give authority to cast out demons? *His apostles and disciples.*
6. What happened when men who were not believers tried to cast out demons and were not believers? *They were attacked and publicly humiliated.*
7. What do we learn about God from these verses? *God gives believers power to cast out demons in the name of Jesus.*

2005

Grapevine Studies
New Testament

Lesson 15
Level 1-2

Mark 1:21-27

Mark 5:1-20

Man in the Synagogue

Man in the Tombs

Luke 9:1-2; 10:17-20

Acts 19:11-20

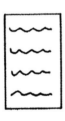

Disciples and Demons

Warning

Lesson Review

1. What is a demon?
2. What is an unclean spirit?
3. What did Jesus do when He encountered people who were possessed with an evil spirit?
4. What did the demons/unclean spirits say about Jesus?
5. To whom did Jesus give authority to cast out demons?
6. What happened when men who were not believers tried to cast out demons and were not believers?
7. What do we learn about God from these verses?

Memory Verse: Luke 9:1

2005

SP 71

Grapevine Studies
Old Testament

C/E Cards
Level 3

JESUS HEALED THE DEMON-POSSESSED

Character/Event Cards

Create a card for Jesus Healed the Demon-Possessed.

- *A demon is spirit who seeks men who will worship it instead of the one true God.*
- *An unclean spirit is an evil spirit that entices men to do evil and is opposed to God.*
- *Jesus rebuked and cast demons out of many people.*
- *Jesus gave His disciples authority over demons.*

Jesus Healed the Demon Possessed

Write your memory verse:

Luke 9:1

Level 2

Memory work: The Twelve Apostles: Andrew, Simon (Peter), Phillip, Matthew (Levi), James, John, *Bartholomew, Thomas, James (son of Alphaeus).*

Grapevine Studies
New Testament

Review
Level 1-2

JESUS RAISED THE DEAD

Timeline Review

Jesus Fed the Multitudes   Healed the Sick   Healed-Demon Possessed

Bible Verses

Luke 9:1

Matthew 4:23

2005

SP 73

Grapevine Studies
New Testament

Lesson 16
Level 1-2

JESUS RAISED THE DEAD

Background Bible Reading: Luke 7-8; John 11
Time Frame: Ministry of Jesus

Jesus and the Widow: *As Jesus entered the town of Nain, he saw a dead man being taken out to be buried who was the only son of his widowed mother. Jesus had compassion on the widow and told her not to weep.*

 widow   *Draw a woman whose son is being carried off.*

Jesus Raised the Dead Man: *Jesus went to the coffin and told the young man to arise. The dead man arose and was returned to his mother. As news spread about this event, the people glorified God.*

 fear   *Draw Jesus returning the young man to his mother.*

Jesus and Jairus: *Jairus came to Jesus to ask Him to come to his home because his only daughter was very sick. Before Jesus could respond, a man came to Jairus and told him that his daughter had died.*

Draw Jairus talking to Jesus.

Jesus Raised the Girl: *Jesus heard what the man said to Jairus, and he told Jairus not to fear. Jesus, along with Peter, James, and John, went with Jairus to his home, where He raised the little girl from the dead.*

Draw a little girl sitting up on a bed.

2005

Grapevine Studies
New Testament

Lesson 16
Level 1-2

JESUS RAISED THE DEAD

Bible Verses: Luke 7:11-17, 8:40-56; John 11:1-45
Time Frame: Ministry of Jesus

Luke 7:11-13

Luke 7:14-17

Jesus and the Widow

Jesus Raised the Dead Man

Luke 8:40-42, 49

Luke 8:50-56

Jesus and Jairus

Jesus Raised the Girl

2005

SP 74

Grapevine Studies
New Testament

Lesson 16
Level 1-2

JESUS RAISED THE DEAD

Word Was Sent to Jesus: *Jesus loved Lazarus and his two sisters, Mary and Martha. When Lazarus became sick, his sisters sent word to Jesus. Lazarus died from the sickness before Jesus arrived.*

 sick   *Draw Mary sending a friend to Jesus.*

Lazarus Died: *By the time Jesus arrived, Lazarus had been in a tomb four days. Jesus talked with Martha, assuring her that Lazarus would indeed be resurrected.*

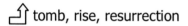 tomb, rise, resurrection   *Draw the tomb and Jesus talking to Martha.*

Jesus Calls Forth Lazarus: *When Jesus arrived at the tomb, He requested that the stone be removed from across the front. Jesus gave thanks and then called Lazarus forth.*

groaning, stone   *Draw Jesus calling into the tomb.*

Lazarus Rose From the Dead: *When Jesus called Lazarus out of the tomb, Lazarus came out of the tomb still wrapped in burial clothes. The Jews who were present with Mary saw that Jesus could raise the dead, and they believed.*

grave clothes, believed   *Draw Lazarus coming forth in grave clothes.*

1. What did Jesus do to the widow's son? *He raised him from the dead.*
2. Why had Jairus come to Jesus? *To request healing for his daughter.*
3. What happened to Jairus's daughter? *She died, and Jesus raised her from the dead.*
4. Who sent for Jesus to tell Him that Lazarus was sick? *His sisters, Mary and Martha.*
5. Where was Lazarus when Jesus arrived in Bethany? *In the tomb.*
6. What happened to Lazarus? *Jesus raised him from the dead.*
7. How did the people respond when Jesus raised people from the dead? *They glorified God, they questioned who Jesus was, and some believed.*
8. What do we learn about God from these verses? *God can raise people from the dead.*

2005

Grapevine Studies
New Testament

Lesson 16
Level 1-2

John 11:1-16

John 11:17-23

Word Sent to Jesus

Lazarus Died

John 11:38-43

John 11:44-45

Jesus Calls Forth Lazarus

Lazarus Rose from the Dead

Lesson Review

1. What did Jesus do to the widow's son?
2. Why had Jairus come to Jesus?
3. What happened to Jairus's daughter?
4. Who sent for Jesus to tell Him that Lazarus was sick?
5. Where was Lazarus when Jesus arrived in Bethany?
6. What happened to Lazarus?
7. How did the people respond when Jesus raised people from the dead?
8. What do we learn about God from these verses?

Memory Verse: Luke 7:15

Grapevine Studies
Old Testament

C/E Cards
Level 3

JESUS RAISED THE DEAD

Character/Event Cards

Create a card for Jesus Raised the Dead.

- *Scripture records that Jesus raised people from the dead including: the widow's son and Jairus' daughter.*
- *Jesus raised Lazarus from the dead after he had been in the tomb four days.*
- *After Lazarus was raised from the dead many Jews believed.*

Jesus Raised the Dead

Write your memory verse:

Luke 7:15

Level 2

Memory work: The Twelve Apostles: Andrew, Simon (Peter), Phillip, Matthew (Levi), James, John, Bartholomew, Thomas, James (son of Alphaeus), *Lebbaeus, Simon (the Canaanite), and Judas Iscariot.*

SP 76

Grapevine Studies
New Testament

Review
Level 1-2

JESUS ENTERED JERUSALEM

Timeline Review

Jesus Healed-Sick   Jesus Healed-Demon Possessed   Raised the Dead

Bible Verses

Luke 7:15

Luke 9:1

2005

SP 77

Grapevine Studies
New Testament

Lesson 17
Level 1-2

JESUS ENTERED JERUSALEM

Background Bible Reading: Matthew 21, John 11-12, Mark 11, Luke 19
Time Frame: The end of Jesus' ministry

The Chief Priests Plotted: *Word spread that Jesus had raised Lazarus from the dead, and many Jews came to see Jesus and Lazarus. Lazarus's resurrection caused many of the Jews to believe. This led the chief priests to plot to kill both Jesus and Lazarus.*

 Chief priest   *Draw a chief priest with frowning faces.*

Jesus Entered Jerusalem: *When Jesus reached the outlying area of Jerusalem, He told two of His disciples to go and bring him back a colt. Jesus rode the colt into Jerusalem, where the people laid leafy branches and their clothes on the road. The people also began to sing and praise Jesus with a song. Jesus was entering Jerusalem to celebrate The Feast of Passover (also called The Feast of Unleavened Bread).*

 hosanna   *Draw Jesus on the colt, and a man waving branches.*

The Pharisees Responded: *When the Pharisees heard the people singing worship songs to Jesus, they demanded that He tell the people to stop. Jesus responded by telling them that if the people were silent, the stones would cry out.*

 Pharisee   *Draw Jesus, the people singing and an angry Pharisee.*

Jesus Wept over Jerusalem: *As Jesus came into Jerusalem, He wept over the city. Throughout Jewish history, the people had been waiting and praying for the coming of the Messiah but when He came, most did not recognize Him.*

Draw Jesus weeping over Jerusalem

2005

Grapevine Studies
New Testament

Lesson 17
Level 1-2

JESUS ENTERED JERUSALEM

Bible Verses: Various
Time Frame: At the end of Jesus' ministry

John 12:9-11

The Chief Priests Plotted

Matt. 21:1-11

Jesus Entered Jerusalem

Luke 19:37-40

The Pharisees Responded

Luke 19:41-44

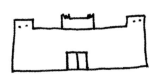

Jesus Wept Over Jerusalem

2005

SP 78

Grapevine Studies
New Testament

Lesson 17
Level 1-2

JESUS ENTERED JERUSALEM

Jesus Cleansed the Temple: *When Jesus entered the temple, He saw people buying and selling instead of praying. Jesus drove out the merchants and money changers and reminded the people that the temple was to be a place of prayer.*

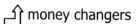 money changers   *Draw Jesus turning over a table.*

Jesus Healed and Children Sang: *After cleansing the temple, Jesus healed the blind and the lame there. The chief priests and scribes heard the children praising Jesus and became indignant.*

 scribes   *Draw Jesus healing and children singing.*

Jesus Taught: *The week preceding the Passover feast, Jesus was in the temple teaching the people and preaching the Gospel (Luke 20:1).*

Draw Jesus teaching a crowd.

The Leaders Plotted: *Although the chief priests, scribes, and leaders of the people wanted to kill Jesus, they were afraid to do so because of the people.*

leaders of the people   *Draw a priest, a scribe, and a leader with frowns.*

1. How did the chief priests respond to Lazarus's resurrection? *They wanted to kill both Jesus and Lazarus.*
2. How did the people respond to Lazarus's resurrection? *Many of the people.*
3. What was Jesus riding when He entered Jerusalem? *A colt that had not been ridden before.*
4. What did the people do when Jesus entered Jerusalem? *They threw leafy branches and coats on the road and sang to Him.*
5. What event brought Jesus to Jerusalem? *The Feast of Passover.*
6. What did Jesus do at the temple? *He drove out the money changers and merchants, then taught and healed.*
7. Why did the leaders hate Jesus? *Because the people believed in Him and followed Him.*
8. What do we learn about God from these verses? *Jesus is God, and He is worthy of both our praise and our prayers.*

2005

Grapevine Studies
New Testament

Lesson 17
Level 1-2

Matt. 21:12-13	Matt. 21:14-16

Jesus Cleansed the Temple	Jesus Healed and Children Sang

Luke 19:47-48

Jesus Taught	The Leaders Plotted

Lesson Review

1. How did the chief priests respond to Lazarus's resurrection?
2. How did the people respond to Lazarus's resurrection?
3. What was Jesus riding when He entered Jerusalem?
4. What did the people do when Jesus entered Jerusalem?
5. What event brought Jesus to Jerusalem?
6. What did Jesus do at the temple?
7. Why did the leaders hate Jesus?
8. What do we learn about God from these verses?

Memory Verse: Matthew 21:9

2005

SP 79

Grapevine Studies
Old Testament

C/E Cards
Level 3

JESUS ENTERED JERUSALEM

Character/Event Cards

Create a card for Jesus Entered Jerusalem.

> - *After Jesus raised Lazarus from the dead the chief priest began plotting how to kill both Jesus and Lazarus.*
> - *When Jesus entered Jerusalem riding on a colt, the people sang and laid their cloaks and leafy branches on the road before Him.*
> - *During the days before the Feast of Passover Jesus removed the moneychangers from the Temple, healed the people, and taught at the Temple.*

Jesus Entered Jerusalem

Write your memory verse:

Matthew 21:9

Level 2

Memory work: The Twelve Apostles: Andrew, Simon (Peter), Phillip, Matthew (Levi), James, John, Bartholomew, Thomas, James (son of Alphaeus), Lebbaeus, Simon (the Canaanite), and Judas Iscariot.

2005

SP 80

Grapevine Studies
New Testament

Review
Level 1-2

THE LAST SUPPER

Timeline Review

Healed- Demon Possessed   Raised the Dead   Jesus Entered Jerusalem

Bible Verses

Matthew 21:9

Luke 7:15

2005

SP 81

Grapevine Studies
New Testament

Lesson 18
Level 1-2

THE LAST SUPPER

Background Bible Reading: Matthew 26; Mark 14; Luke 21; John 13
Time Frame: The night before Jesus was crucified

Jesus Warned of His Death: *During the week of Passover, Jesus warned His disciples that soon He was going to be killed. The chief priests, scribes, and elders gathered with the high priest to plot how to kill Jesus by devious means.*

 Passover   *Draw Jesus, thinking of the cross, and one of His disciples.*

Judas and the Chief Priest: *As Passover drew near, Satan entered the apostle named Judas (Iscariot) to betray Jesus. Judas met with the chief priests to arrange for the betrayal. Judas was paid for his part in the scheme.*

Draw a chief priest handing Judas money.

Passover Preparations: *On the first day of the Feast of Passover Jesus gave directions to His Disciples regarding the upcoming Passover meal.*

Draw the disciples setting a table.

Judas Was Identified as the Betrayer: *At the Last Supper, Jesus revealed Judas as the betrayer.*

Draw Jesus dipping His hand into a bowl with Judas.

2005

Grapevine Studies
New Testament

Lesson 18
Level 1-2

THE LAST SUPPER

Bible Verses: Matthew 26:1-35; Luke 22:1-6; John 13:1-17
Time Frame: The night before Jesus was crucified

Matt. 26:1-5	Luke 22:1-6

Jesus Warned of His Death

Judas and the Chief Priest

Matt. 26:17-19	Matt. 26:20-25

Passover Preparations

Judah Was Identified as the Betrayer

2005

SP 82

Grapevine Studies
New Testament

Lesson 18
Level 1-2

THE LAST SUPPER

The Last Supper: *Toward the end of the Last Supper, Jesus blessed the bread and the cup, instituting the New Covenant. After the meal Jesus and His apostles sang a hymn and went to the Mount of Olives.*

Draw Judas leaving.

All Would Stumble: *Jesus warned the apostles and then quoted a prophecy which stated that all His "flock" would be scattered and would stumble because of the events which were about to take place.*

 stumble

Draw Jesus talking with the disciples.

Peter's Statement: *Peter denied that he would stumble, but Jesus told him that before the night was finished Peter would deny Him three times.*

Draw Jesus and Peter pointing to himself.

1. What did Jesus tell His apostles regarding His death? *He would be killed.*
2. With whom did Judas conspire? *The chief priest, the captain, the scribes, and the Pharisees.*
3. What feast did Jesus and His apostles celebrate? *The Feast of Passover.*
4. What did Jesus institute with the cup and the bread on the night of the Last Supper? *The New Covenant.*
5. Which apostle did Jesus identify as the one who would betray Him? *Judas.*
6. What did Judas get in exchange for his betrayal? *Money.*
7. What did Jesus tell His apostles they would do later that night? *They would stumble and scatter.*
8. What did Peter proclaim? *He would not deny the Lord.*
9. What do we learn about God from these verses? *Jesus was committed to God's plan of bringing forth in the New Covenant.*

2005

Grapevine Studies
New Testament

Lesson 18
Level 1-2

Matt. 26:26-29

The Last Supper

Matt. 26:30-32

Matt. 26:33-35

All would Stumble

Peter's Statement

Lesson Review

1. What did Jesus tell His apostles regarding His death?
2. With whom did Judas conspire?
3. What feast did Jesus and His apostles celebrate?
4. What did Jesus cup and the bread and on the night of the Last Supper?
5. Which apostle did Jesus identify as the one who would betray Him?
6. What did Judas get in exchange for his betrayal?
7. What did Jesus tell His apostles they would do later that night?
8. What did Peter proclaim?
9. What do we learn about God from these verses?

Memory Verse: John 13:1

2005

SP 83

Grapevine Studies
New Testament

Review 3
Level 1-2

Review 3

1. When Jesus asked the disciple to feed the crowds, how did they respond? *By telling Jesus that they didn't have enough food to feed the crowds.*
2. What did Jesus do with the fish and loaves? *He gave thanks and blessed the loaves and fish.*
3. How many people did Jesus feed with five loaves and two fish? *5,000 men.*
4. How many people did Jesus feed with seven loaves and a few small fish? *4,000 men.*
5. Recite Luke 9:16.
6. What kinds of sicknesses and ailments did Jesus heal? *The deaf, mute, blind, lepers, and those with palsy.*
7. Where did Jesus heal? *In various cities, on the roadways, and in homes.*
8. What was the response of some of those who were healed? *They thanked Jesus and worshipped and praised God.*
9. How did the scribes respond to Jesus healing people and forgiving them of their sins? *They questioned Jesus' authority to forgive sins.*
10. Recite Matthew 4:23.
11. What is a demon? *A spirit who seeks men who will worship it instead of the one true God.*
12. What is an unclean spirit? *Evil spirit who entices men to do evil and is opposed to God.*
13. What did Jesus do when He encountered people who were possessed with an evil spirit? *He rebuked and then cast out the demon/evil spirit.*
14. What did the demons/unclean spirits say about Jesus? *They called Him the Holy One of God and The Son of the Most High God.*
15. To whom did Jesus give authority to cast out demons? *His apostles and disciples.*
16. What happened to the men who were not believers when they tried to cast out demon? *They were attacked and publicly humiliated.*
17. Recite Luke 9:1.
18. What did Jesus do to the widow's son? *He raised him from the dead.*
19. Why had Jairus come to Jesus? *To request healing for his daughter.*

2005

SP 84

20. What happened to Jairus's daughter? *She died, and Jesus came and raised her from the dead.*
21. Who sent for Jesus to tell Him that Lazarus was sick? *His sisters, Mary and Martha.*
22. Where was Lazarus when Jesus arrived in Bethany? *In the tomb.*
23. What happened to Lazarus? *Jesus raised him from the dead.*
24. How did the people respond when Jesus raised people from the dead? *The glorified God, they questioned who Jesus was, and some believed in Jesus.*
25. Recite Luke 7:15.
26. How did the chief priests respond to Lazarus's resurrection? *They wanted to kill both Jesus and Lazarus.*
27. How did the people respond to Lazarus's resurrection? *The people believed in Jesus.*
28. What was Jesus riding when He entered Jerusalem? *A colt that had not been ridden before.*
29. What did the people do when Jesus entered Jerusalem? *They threw leafy branches and coats in the road and sang to Him.*
30. What event brought Jesus to Jerusalem? *The Feast of Passover.*
31. What did Jesus do at the temple? *He drove out the moneychangers and merchants, then taught and healed.*
32. Why did the leaders hate Jesus? *Because the people believed in Him and followed Him.*
33. Recite Matthew 21:9.
34. What did Jesus tell His apostles regarding His death? *He would be crucified.*
35. With whom did Judas conspire? *The chief priest, the captain, the scribes, and the Pharisees.*
36. What feast did Jesus and His apostles celebrate? *The Feast of Passover.*
37. What did Jesus institute with the cup and the bread on the night of the Last Supper? *The New Covenant.*
38. Which apostle did Jesus identify as the one who would betray Him? *Judas.*
39. What did Judas get in exchange for his betrayal? *Money.*
40. What did Jesus tell His apostles they would do later that night? *They would stumble and scatter.*
41. What did Peter proclaim? *He would not deny the Lord.*
42. Recite John 13:1.

Mid-Series Review

Grapevine Studies
New Testament

Mid-Series Review
Level 1-2

New Testament Timeline

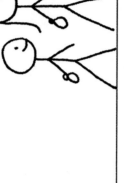

| Birth of John | Birth of Jesus | Jesus in Egypt | Jesus at Age Twelve |

Recite or write out the following verses on a separate sheet of paper.

1. Luke 1:80
2. Galatians 4:4-5
3. Matthew 2:11
4. Luke 2:52

SP 86

Grapevine Studies
New Testament

Mid-Series Review
Level 1-2

New Testament Timeline

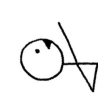

| John Prepared the Way | The Baptism of Jesus | Temptation of Jesus | The Twelve Apostles |

5. Mark 1:9

6. Hebrews 4:15

7. Revelation 20:10

8. Matthew 28:19-20

Grapevine Studies
New Testament

Mid-Series Review
Level 1-2

New Testament Timeline

| Jesus Taught | Jesus Prayed | Jesus Calmed the Sea | Jesus Fed the Multitudes |

9. Matthew 22:37-39

10. Mark 1:35

11. Matthew 8:27

12. Luke 9:16

SP 88

Grapevine Studies
New Testament

Mid-Series Review
Level 1-2

New Testament Timeline

Jesus Healed the Sick/Lame

Jesus Healed the Demon-Possessed

Jesus Raised the Dead

13. Matthew 4:23

14. Luke 9:1

15. Luke 7:15

Grapevine Studies
New Testament

Mid-Series Review
Level 1-2

New Testament Timeline

Jesus Entered Jerusalem

The Last Supper

16. Matthew 21:9
17. John 13:1

Level 2

18. Name the books of the New Testament. *Matthew, Mark, Luke John, Acts, Romans, I & II Corinthians, Galatians, Ephesians, Philippians, Colossians, I & II Thessalonians, I & II Timothy, Titus, Philemon, Hebrews, James, I & II Peter, I, II & III John, Jude, and Revelation.*

19. Name The Twelve Apostles. *Andrew, Simon (Peter), Phillip, Matthew (Levi), James, John, Bartholomew, Thomas, James (son of Alphaeus), Lebbaeus, Simon (the Canaanite), and Judas Iscariot.*

SP 90

My Notes on the Timeline:

Section 5 Goals and Key Points

THE GARDEN OF GETHSEMANE

The goal of this lesson is to see what took place in the Garden of Gethsemane.

Key Points:
- After the Last Supper, Jesus and the eleven apostles went to the Garden to pray.
- Jesus prayed that not His will but the Father's will would be done.
- While Jesus prayed the apostles slept.
- Judas betrayed Jesus in the garden.
- Jesus healed the servant's ear that was cut off by Peter.
- When Jesus was arrested the apostles fled.

THE TRIALS OF JESUS

The goal of this lesson is to trace the three religious trials that Jesus went through on the last night of His life.

Key Points:
- Jesus was taken to Annas for His first trial.
- Jesus was taken to Caiaphas for His second trial.
- Peter denied Jesus three times.
- Jesus was beaten and mocked.
- Jesus was taken before Caiaphas and the Council, where He was condemned on the charge of blasphemy.

JESUS WAS CONDEMNED TO DEATH

The goal of this lesson is to trace the three civil trials that Jesus went through on the last night of His life.

Key Points:
- After Jesus was condemned by the Council, He was taken to Pilate to be questioned.
- Pilate sent Jesus to Herod Antipas after he found no fault in Him.
- Herod returned Jesus to Pilate.
- Pilate released Barabbas at the request of the crowd.
- Pilate washed his hands before the crowd to indicate that he did not believe that Jesus was worthy of death.
- Jesus was then scourged and beaten.

THE CRUCIFIXION

The goal of this lesson is to establish the fact that Jesus was crucified and died.

Key Points:
- Simon carried Jesus' crossbeam to the place of execution.
- The inscription above Jesus read, "This is the King of the Jews."
- Jesus was crucified between two thieves.
- Jesus asked God to forgive those involved in His death.
- The soldiers cast lots for Jesus' clothing.
- The crowd mocked Jesus while he was on the cross.

THE DEATH OF JESUS

The goal of this lesson is to examine the events surrounding the death of Jesus.

Key Points:
- Jesus asked the apostle John to care for His mother.
- Jesus cried out to God and then died.
- When Jesus died three things happened:
    1. The temple veil was torn top to bottom.
    2. An earthquake struck.
    3. Saints were resurrected.
- A soldier pierced His side to confirm His death.

THE BURIAL AND RESURRECTION

The goal of this lesson is to understand the events that occurred at the burial and resurrection of Jesus.

Key Points:
- Jesus was buried by Joseph of Arimathea and Nicodemus.
- Jesus was buried in a new tomb.
- A guard was set at the tomb to insure that the disciples did not steal the body.
- After three days Jesus rose from the grave.
- Mary, Peter, and the disciples verified the resurrection by confirming that the tomb was empty.

Grapevine Studies
Old Testament

C/E Cards
Level 3

THE LAST SUPPER

Character/Event Cards

Create a card for the Last Supper.

- *Jesus warned His Apostles that He would be killed.*
- *The chief priest plotted with Judas Iscariot for Jesus' arrest.*
- *Jesus ate the Last Supper with all of His Apostles.*
- *Jesus warned His Apostles that they would all stumble.*

The Last Supper

Write your memory verse:

John 13:1

Level 2

Memory Work: *Introduce the Apostle's Creed. See page 307.*

Dear Teacher: Memory work during the last half of this series will be the memorizing of The Apostle's Creed. We are using the Modern English Version. We recommend a brief explanation of the history and development of this creed.

2005

SP 94

Grapevine Studies
New Testament

Review
Level 1-2

THE GARDEN OF GETHSEMANE

Timeline Review

Jesus Raised the Dead   Jesus Entered Jerusalem   Last Supper

Bible Verses

John 13:1

Matthew 21:9

2005

SP 95

Grapevine Studies
New Testament

Lesson 19
Level 1-2

THE GARDEN OF GETHSEMANE

Background Bible Reading: Matthew 26; Mark 14; Luke 22; John 18
Time Frame: The last night of Jesus' earthly life

Jesus Went to Gethsemane: *After the Last Supper Jesus took His disciples and went to the Garden of Gethsemane, which was His custom. Upon arriving at the garden, Jesus took Peter, James, and John aside and asked them to watch and pray with Him.*

 tempted   *Draw Jesus in the Garden of Gethsemane.*

Not My Will But Yours: *Jesus went a little farther into the garden and prayed not that His own will would be done, but that the Father's will would be done.*

 will   *Draw Jesus praying.*

Jesus Was Strengthened: *While Jesus prayed, an angel appeared and strengthened Him.*

 strengthened   *Draw an angel with Jesus.*

The Disciples Slept: *Jesus prayed so earnestly that He sweat drops of blood. After a time of prayer, He returned to His disciples to find them sleeping. After awaking them and exhorting them, He went again to pray. A second time He returned to find them asleep.*

Draw Jesus standing and a disciple sleeping.

2005

Grapevine Studies
New Testament

Lesson 19
Level 1-2

THE GARDEN OF GETHSEMANE

Bible Verses: Mark 14:32-51; Luke 22:39-53; John 18:1-11
Time Frame: The last night of Jesus' earthly life

Mark 14:32-34

Mark 14:35-36

Jesus Went to Gethsemane

Not My Will But Yours

Luke 22:43

Mark 14:37-42

Jesus Was Strengthened

The Disciples Slept

2005

SP 96

Grapevine Studies
New Testament

Lesson 19
Level 1-2

THE GARDEN OF GETHSEMANE

Judas Went to the Garden: *After leaving the Last Supper, Judas went to the chief priest. Judas took with him a great crowd (the chief priest, the elders, and the officers of the temple), and went to the garden, where He betrayed Jesus with a kiss.*

 I AM   *Draw Jesus and Judas.*

Jesus Healed the Servant's Ear: *Peter, in an attempt to defend Jesus, struck out with his sword and cut off the ear of the servant of the high priest. Jesus rebuked Peter and healed the servant's ear.*

Draw man whose ear was healed.

Jesus Questioned His Arrest: *Jesus asked the crowd who they were looking for, and upon their response, He asked why they had waited to arrest Him when He had been regularly in the temple.*

Draw Jesus questioning a chief priest.

The Disciples Fled: *When Jesus' disciples saw what was happening, they all fled.*

Draw the disciples fleeing.

1. Where did Jesus take His disciples to pray? *The Garden of Gethsemane.*
2. What did Jesus pray? *Not, His own will would be done but that the Father's will would be done.*
3. Who strengthened Jesus in the garden? *An angel.*
4. What did the disciples do while Jesus prayed? *They slept.*
5. Who was included in the crowd that went to the garden to arrest Jesus? *Judas, the chief priests, officers of the temple, and the elders.*
6. Who did Jesus heal? *The servant of the high priest.*
7. What did the disciples do when Jesus was arrested? *They fled.*
8. What do we learn about God from these verses? *God's will is to be done even when it is not our will.*

2005

Grapevine Studies
New Testament

Lesson 19
Level 1-2

| John 18:1-6 | Luke 22:49-51 |

Judas Went to the Garden — Jesus Healed the Servant's Ear

| Luke 22:52-53 | Mark 14:50 |
| Mark 14:48-49 | |

Jesus Questioned His Arrest — The Disciples Fled

Lesson Review

1. Where did Jesus take His disciples to pray?
2. What did Jesus pray?
3. Who strengthened Jesus in the garden?
4. What did the disciples do while Jesus prayed?
5. Who was included in the crowd that went to the garden to arrest Jesus?
6. Who did Jesus heal?
7. What did the disciples do when Jesus was arrested?
8. What do we learn about God from these verses?

Memory Verse: Mark 14:36

Grapevine Studies
Old Testament

C/E Cards
Level 3

THE GARDEN OF GETHSEMANE

Character/Event Cards

Create a card for the Garden of Gethsemane.

- After the Passover Meal Jesus and the 11 Apostles went to the Garden.
- While Jesus prayed the Apostles fell asleep.
- Jesus prayed not His will but that the will of the Father would be done.
- Judas betrayed Jesus.
- After Peter cut off the ear of the servant, Jesus healed the servant's ear.
- When Jesus was arrested the Apostles fled.

The Garden of Gethsemane

Write your memory verse:

Mark 14:36

Level 2

Memory Work: Continue to memorize the Apostle's Creed.

2005

SP 98

Grapevine Studies
New Testament

Review
Level 1-2

THE TRIALS OF JESUS

Timeline Review

Jesus Entered Jerusalem   Last Supper   Garden of Gethsemane

Bible Verses

Mark 14:36

John 13:1

Grapevine Studies
New Testament

Lesson 20
Level 1-2

THE TRIALS OF JESUS

Background Bible Reading: Matthew 26-27; Mark 15; Luke 22; John 18
Time Frame: The night and morning before Jesus was crucified

Trial 1: Annas: *After Jesus was arrested He was taken to Annas, the high priest, for His first trial. Annas asked him about His disciples and doctrine. Jesus responded that His teaching (doctrine) was always in the open and those who heard Him could bear witness to His teaching.*

👆 high priest, doctrine *Draw Jesus before Annas.*

Trial 2: Caiaphas, the High Priest: *Annas had Jesus bound and sent to Caiaphas for trial.*

Draw Jesus before Caiaphas.

Peter Denied Jesus: *Peter followed Jesus and his captors to the home of the high priest. While Peter was standing in the courtyard, three people recognized him as one of the disciples of Jesus, and three times Peter denied their statements adamantly. Jesus looked at Peter just as he was giving his third denial, and at that moment a rooster crowed.*

Draw Peter saying "No!" when questioned by a man.

Jesus Was Beaten and Mocked: *As Jesus was held in the courtyard of the high priest's home the men who held Him beat and mocked Jesus.*

👆 mocked, blasphemously *Draw Jesus being beat and mocked.*

2005

Grapevine Studies
New Testament

Lesson 20
Level 1-2

THE TRIALS OF JESUS

Bible Verses: Matthew 26:59 -27:10; Luke 22:54-72; John 18:12-24
Time Frame: The night and morning before Jesus was crucified

John 18:12-14, 19-23

Trial 1: Annas

John 18:24

Trial 2: Caiaphas, High Priest

Luke 22:54-62

"NO!"

Peter Denied Jesus

Luke 22:63-65

Jesus Was Beaten and Mocked

2005

SP 100

Grapevine Studies
New Testament

Lesson 20
Level 1-2

THE TRIALS OF JESUS

Trial 3: Caiaphas and the Council: *Caiaphas had Jesus taken before the chief priests, the scribes and the elders to be tried. False witnesses were brought to testify against Jesus, and finally the high priest asked Him if He was the Christ, to which Jesus responded that He was.*

⤴ chief priests, scribes, elders   *Draw Jesus before Caiaphas and the Council.*

The Council Condemned Jesus: *When Jesus told the Council that He was the Christ, the high priest tore his clothes and accused Jesus of speaking blasphemy. The Council then demanded that Jesus be put to death. Jesus was then taken to Pilate.*

 Pilate   *Draw a member of the Council condemning Jesus.*

Judas Died: *When Judas heard that the Council had condemned Jesus to death, he was sorry. Judas sought to return the money to the priests. Judas then went and hanged himself. The chief priests consulted together and used the blood money to buy a field.*

Draw Judas's grave.

1. Who conducted the first trial of Jesus? *Annas.*
2. Who conducted the second trial of Jesus? *Caiaphas.*
3. What did Peter do when questioned about whether he was a disciple? *He denied it three times.*
4. What did the soldiers do to Jesus? *They beat and mocked him.*
5. Who conducted the third trial of Jesus? *Caiaphas and The Council/The Sanhedrin.*
6. What crime did the Council accuse Jesus of committing? *Blasphemy.*
7. What happened to Judas? *He hanged himself.*
8. What do we learn about God from these verses? *God is with us even when our closest friends abandon us.*

2005

Grapevine Studies
New Testament

Mark 14:55-62

Lesson 20
Level 1-2

Trial 3: Caiaphas and the

Mark 14:63-65

Matt. 27:3-5

Matt. 27:1-2

  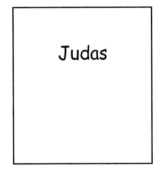

The Council Condemned Jesus

Judas Died

Lesson Review

1. Who conducted the first trial of Jesus?
2. Who conducted the second trial of Jesus?
3. What did Peter do when questioned about whether he was a disciple?
4. What did the soldiers do to Jesus?
5. Who conducted the third trial of Jesus?
6. What crime did the Council accuse Jesus of committing?
7. What happened to Judas?
8. What do we learn about God from these verses?

Memory Verse: Matthew 26:57

2005

SP 101

Grapevine Studies
Old Testament

C/E Cards
Level 3

THE TRIALS OF JESUS

Character/Event Cards

Create a card for the Trials of Jesus.

> - *Jesus had three religious trials:*
>   1. *Annas*
>   2. *Caiaphas*
>   3. *Caiaphas and The Council.*
> - *Peter denied Jesus three times during these trials.*
> - *Jesus was beaten and mocked.*
> - *Jesus was condemned to death on the charge of blasphemy.*

The Trials of Jesus

Write your memory verse:

Matthew 26:57

Level 2

Memory Work: Continue to memorize the Apostle's Creed.

2005

SP 102

Grapevine Studies
New Testament

Review
Level 1-2

JESUS WAS CONDEMNED TO DEATH

Timeline Review

Last Supper   Garden of Gethsemane   Jesus Arrested

Bible Verses

Matthew 26:57

Mark 14:36

SP 103

Grapevine Studies
New Testament

Lesson 21
Level 1-2

JESUS WAS CONDEMNED TO DEATH

Background Bible Reading: John 18-19
Time Frame: The last morning of Jesus' earthly life

Trial 4: Pilate: *After being tried by the Sanhedrin, the crowd took Jesus to Pilate (at the Antonia Fortress). At this point the accusations against Jesus changed from those related to the Jewish law to those related to Roman law. Pilate found no fault in Jesus, and when he learned that Jesus was from Galilee, Pilate sent Him to Herod.*

 fault   *Draw Pilate, Jesus, and the crowd yelling accusations.*

Trial 5: Herod Antipas: *Herod was pleased that Jesus was brought to him, for Herod had wanted to see Jesus, whom he had heard much about. Although Herod questioned Jesus, Jesus did not answer any of the questions. After questioning Jesus, he sent Him back to Pilate.*

 Herod Antipas   *Draw Jesus before Herod.*

Trial 6: Pilate Questioned Jesus: *After appearing before Herod, Jesus was returned to Pilate for His final trial. Pilate asked Jesus if He was the King of the Jews, and Jesus responded that He was the King of the Jews. The chief priests and the elders began accusing Him before Pilate, but Jesus did not answer their accusations.*

 governor   *Draw Jesus before Pilate, and the chief priests and elders accusing Him.*

Barabbas or Jesus: *Pilate had a tradition of releasing a prisoner at the Feast of Passover. When Pilate asked the crowd whom they wanted released, at the prompting of the chief priests and elders, the crowd demanded a criminal named Barabbas. It is interesting to note that Pilate's wife had a dream and warned Pilate to have nothing to do with Jesus.*

Draw Jesus standing before Pilate.

2005

Grapevine Studies
New Testament

Lesson 21
Level 1-2

JESUS WAS CONDEMNED TO DEATH

Bible Verses: Matthew 27:11-31; Mark 15:6-20; Luke 23:1-12
Time Frame: The last morning of Jesus' earthly life

Luke 23:1-7

Luke 23:8-12

Trial 4: Pilate

Trial 5: Herod Antipas

Matt. 27:11-14

Matt. 27:15-21

Trial 6: Pilate Questioned Jesus

Barabbas or Jesus

2005

SP 104

Grapevine Studies
New Testament

Lesson 21
Level 1-2

JESUS WAS CONDEMNED TO DEATH

Pilate Washed His Hands: *When Pilate asked the crowd what he should do with Jesus, they demanded that Pilate should have Jesus crucified. Although Pilate did not think that Jesus was guilty, his desire was to please the crowd and prevent a riot.*

 washing his hands, just   *Draw Pilate washing his hands.*

Jesus Was Scourged: *Pilate released Barabbas and turned Jesus over to be scourged and then crucified.*

 scourged   *Draw Jesus being scourged.*

Jesus Was Beaten: *After being scourged Jesus was clothed in a scarlet/purple robe and had a crown of thorns placed on His head. After beating and spitting on Jesus, the soldiers removed the robe and dressed Him in His own clothes.*

 garrison, mocked   *Draw Jesus with a crown of thorns and a robe on, a soldier mocking.*

1. Who tried Jesus after the Council? *Pontius Pilate.*
2. Why did Pilate send Jesus to Herod? *Jesus was from Herod's district.*
3. Who tried Jesus last? *Pontius Pilate.*
4. Who was Barabbas? *A criminal released by Pilate during the Feast of Passover.*
5. Why did Pilate wash his hands? *To make the statement that he was innocent in the death of Jesus.*
6. What did the soldiers do to Jesus? *They scourged Him, beat Him, put a scarlet/purple robe and a crown of thorns on Him, and then mocked Him.*
7. What do we learn about God from these verses? *Jesus stated that He was the King of the Jews.*

2005

Grapevine Studies
New Testament

Lesson 21
Level 1-2

Matt. 27:22-25
Mark 15:12-14

Matt. 27:26
Mark 15:15

Pilate Washed His Hands

Jesus Was Scourged

Matt. 27:27-31

Jesus Was Beaten

Lesson Review

1. Who tried Jesus after the Council?
2. Why did Pilate send Jesus to Herod?
3. Who tried Jesus last?
4. Who was Barabbas?
5. Why did Pilate wash his hands?
6. What did the soldiers do to Jesus?
7. What do we learn about God from these verses?

Memory Verse: Matthew 27:26

2005

SP 105

Grapevine Studies
Old Testament

C/E Cards
Level 3

JESUS WAS CONDEMNED TO DEATH

Character/Event Cards

Create a card for Jesus was Condemned to Death.

> - Jesus had three civil trials:
>   1. Pontus Pilate
>   2. Herod Antipas
>   3. Pontus Pilate
> - Pilate declared Jesus innocent but condemned Him to death at the crowd's request.
> - Barabbas was released instead of Jesus.
> - Jesus was beaten and mocked with a robe and crown of thrones before being scourged.

Jesus was Condemned to Death

Write your memory verse:

Matthew 27:26

Level 2

Memory Work: Continue to memorize the Apostle's Creed.

2005

SP 106

THE CRUCIFIXION

Timeline Review

Garden of Gethsemane   *Jesus Arrested*   *Jesus Tried and Condemned*

Bible Verses

Matthew 27:26

Matthew 26:57

Grapevine Studies
New Testament

Lesson 22
Level 1-2

THE CRUCIFIXION

Background Bible Reading: Matthew 27; Mark 15; Luke 23; John 19
Time Frame: The last hours of Jesus' earthly life

Simon Carried the Cross: *After Jesus was scourged and beaten, He was led away to be crucified. Because of Jesus' weakened condition, He was unable to carry His crossbeam to the place of execution, so Simon of Cyrene carried the crossbeam for Jesus. As Jesus was led out through the multitude, He spoke to those that followed Him and warned them of the events to come. Two other criminals were also led out with Jesus to be crucified.*

Draw Jesus stumbling along and Simon carrying the crossbeam.

The Inscription: *Above each crucified person an inscription was placed indicating the type of crime he had been charged with. Pilate wrote Jesus' inscription, and the chief priests protested, but Pilate refused to have the inscription changed.*

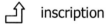 inscription   *Write the inscription that was above Jesus.*

Jesus Was Crucified: *Jesus was crucified around 9:00 A.M. at a place called Golgotha, outside the city of Jerusalem. I recommend that teachers do a personal study on this most important event to determine what their students should know.*

 crucified   *Draw Jesus hanging on the cross.*

2005

Grapevine Studies
New Testament

Lesson 22
Level 1-2

THE CRUCIFIXION

Bible Verses: Matthew 27:33-44; Mark 15:22-32; Luke 23:26-43; John 19:19-24
Time Frame: The last hours of Jesus' life

Luke 23:26-28, 32

John 19:19-22

Jesus of Nazareth

The King of the Jews

Simon Carried the Cross

The Inscription

Matt. 27:33-38

Mark 15:22-28

Luke 23:33

John 19:17-18

Jesus Was Crucified

THE CRUCIFIXION

**Lesson 22
Level 1-2**

Forgiveness: *On the cross, Jesus prayed that the Father would forgive those who had crucified Him.*

 forgive   *Draw Jesus praying on the cross.*

The Soldiers: *After Jesus was crucified the soldiers cast lots for His clothing, as had been prophesied.*

 tunic, lots   *Draw a soldier holding the winning lot and a tunic.*

The Crowd Mocked: *The soldiers, thieves, chief priests, scribes, elders, and those passing by the cross mocked Jesus.*

 mocked, sour wine   *Draw the priests, men, and women mocking Jesus.*

The Thieves: *One of the crucified thieves mocked Jesus, while the other thief recognized his own sin and the innocence of Jesus. The repentant thief asked Jesus to remember him, and Jesus assured this thief that he would be with Jesus in Paradise.*

blasphemed, Paradise   *Draw Jesus speaking to one of the thieves.*

1. Who carried the cross for Jesus? *Simon of Cyrene.*
2. What inscription did Pilate have put above Jesus? *Jesus of Nazareth, the King of the Jews.*
3. What happened to Jesus at Golgotha? *He was crucified.*
4. What did Jesus ask the Father to do to those who crucified Him? *Forgive them.*
5. Who cast lots for Jesus' tunic? *The soldiers who crucified Him.*
6. What did the crowd do to Jesus while He was on the cross? *They mocked Him.*
7. What did Jesus promise the repentant thief on the cross? *He would be with Jesus that day in Paradise.*
8. What do we learn about God from these verses? *God is a forgiving God, and Jesus suffered a great deal for the penalty of our sins.*

Grapevine Studies
New Testament

Lesson 22
Level 1-2

Luke 23:33-34

John 19:23-24

Forgiveness

The Soldiers

Matt. 27:39-44

Luke 23:35-37

Luke 23:39-43

The Crowd Mocked

The Thieves

Lesson Review

1. Who carried the cross for Jesus?
2. What inscription did Pilate have put above Jesus?
3. What happened to Jesus at Golgotha?
4. What did Jesus ask the Father to do to those who crucified Him?
5. Who cast lots for Jesus' tunic?
6. What did the crowd do to Jesus while He was on the cross?
7. What did Jesus promise the repentant thief on the cross?
8. What do we learn about God from these verses?

Memory Verse: Luke 23:33

2005

SP 109

Grapevine Studies
Old Testament

C/E Cards
Level 3

THE CRUCIFIXION

Character/Event Cards

Create a card for the Crucifixion.

- *Simon carried the cross for Jesus.*
- *The inscription on the cross read, "This is the King of the Jews."*
- *Jesus was crucified between two thieves.*
- *Jesus asked God to forgive those involved in His death.*
- *The soldiers cast lots for Jesus' clothing.*
- *The crowd mocked Jesus on the cross.*

The Crucifixion

Write your memory verse:

Luke 23:33

Level 2

Memory Work: Continue to memorize the Apostle's Creed.

2005

SP 110

Grapevine Studies　　　　　　　　　　　　　　　　　　　　Review
New Testament　　　　　　　　　　　　　　　　　　　　　Level 1-2

THE DEATH OF JESUS

Timeline Review

Garden of Gethsemane　　　Jesus Tried and Condemned　　　Jesus Crucified

Bible Verses

Luke 23:33

Matthew 27:26

2005　　　　　　　　　　　　　　　　　　　　　　　　SP 111

Grapevine Studies
New Testament

Lesson 23
Level 1-2

THE DEATH OF JESUS

Background Bible Reading: Matthew 27; Mark 15; Luke 23; John 19
Time Frame: The end of Jesus' earthly life

Jesus, John, and Mary: *While on the cross Jesus made provisions for His mother to be cared for by the Apostle John.*

Draw Jesus on the cross, John, and Mary.

Jesus Cried Out to God: *From the sixth hour to the ninth hour, darkness covered the land. The last thing that Jesus did before He died was to cry out to the Father.*

 sixth/ninth hour   *Draw Jesus crying out.*

Jesus Died: *Jesus knew that He had accomplished all that needed to be completed, and then He stated "It is finished" and gave up His spirit.*

finished   *Draw Jesus dead on the cross.*

Grapevine Studies
New Testament

Lesson 23
Level 1-2

THE DEATH OF JESUS

Bible Verses: Matthew 27:50-53; Mark 15:33-39; Luke 23:44-47; John 19:25-37
Time Frame: The end of Jesus' earthly life

John 19:25-27

Mark 15:33-36

Luke 23:44-46

Jesus, John and Mary

Jesus Cried Out to God

John 19:28-30

Mark 15:37

Jesus Died

2005

SP 112

Grapevine Studies
New Testament

Lesson 23
Level 1-2

THE DEATH OF JESUS

The Temple Veil: *Many important and interesting events surrounded the death of Jesus. The darkness lifted and the Veil in the temple (separating the Holy of Holies from the Most Holy Place) was torn top to bottom.*

temple veil — *Draw the temple veil hanging in two pieces.*

The Earthquake: *An earthquake struck Jerusalem.*

Draw the earth shaking.

The Graves Opened: *The graves of dead saints opened, and they were resurrected and appeared to many.*

fallen asleep — *Draw people coming out of graves.*

The Centurion: *After witnessing the death of Jesus and the events surrounding His death, the centurions and guards were very afraid and proclaimed that Jesus must have been the "Son of God."*

centurion — *Draw the centurion pointing.*

Jesus Was Pierced: *As evening approached it was necessary to remove the bodies from the crosses in order to bury them before sundown. To hasten the death of those being crucified, the legs of both thieves were broken. However, when they came to break Jesus' legs it was discovered that He was already dead. To ensure that He was dead, a spear was thrust into His side, bringing forth water and blood.*

Preparation Day — *Draw Jesus being pierced.*

1. Whom did Jesus tell to take care of His mother? *John.*
2. What three things happened at the death of Jesus? *(1) The temple veil was torn in two, (2) an earthquake struck, and (3) the graves of the saints were opened and they appeared to many.*
3. Upon His death had Jesus completed the work given to Him by God the Father? *Yes.*
4. Who proclaimed at Jesus' death that He was the "Son of God"? *The centurion.*
5. Why did the soldier pierce Jesus' side? *To make sure He was dead.*
6. What do we learn about God from these verses? *Jesus fulfilled all of the things prophesied about the Messiah, and He completed the work given to Him by God.*

2005

Grapevine Studies
New Testament

Lesson 23
Level 1-2

Matt. 27:50-53

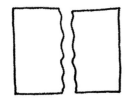 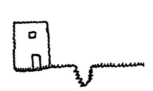 

The Temple Veil   The Earthquake   The Graves Opened

Matt. 27:54
Mark 15:37-39

John 19:31-37

The Centurion   Jesus Was Pierced

Lesson Review

1. Whom did Jesus tell to take care of His mother?
2. What three things happened at the death of Jesus?
3. Upon His death, had Jesus completed the work given to Him by God the Father?
4. Who proclaimed at Jesus' death that He was the "Son of God"?
5. Why did the soldier pierce Jesus' side?
6. What do we learn about God from these verses?

Memory Verse: Luke 23:46

Grapevine Studies
Old Testament

C/E Cards
Level 3

THE DEATH OF JESUS

Character/Event Cards

Create a card for the Death of Jesus.

> - *Jesus asked the Apostle John to care for His mother.*
> - *Jesus cried out to God and then died.*
> - *A soldier pierced Jesus side to confirm that He was dead.*
> - *When Jesus died three things happened:*
>   1. *The Temple Veil was torn top to bottom.*
>   2. *An earthquake struck.*
>   3. *Saints were resurrected.*
> - *A soldier pierced Jesus side to confirm that He was dead.*

The Death of Jesus

Write your memory verse:

Luke 23:46

Level 2

Memory Work: Continue to memorize the Apostle's Creed.

2005

SP 114

Grapevine Studies
New Testament

Review
Level 1-2

THE BURIAL AND RESURRECTION

Timeline Review

Jesus Tried and Condemned *Jesus Crucified* Jesus Died

Bible Verses

Luke 23:46

Luke 23:33

Grapevine Studies
New Testament

Lesson 24
Level 1-2

THE BURIAL AND RESURRECTION

Background Bible Reading: Matthew 27-28; Luke 23-2; John 19-20
Time Frame: After the death of Jesus on the cross

Jesus Was Buried: *Joseph of Arimathea, (a member of the Council who was a rich man and a secret follower of Jesus) went to Pilate and received permission to take the body of Jesus. Joseph and Nicodemus wrapped Jesus' body in linen and laid him in Joseph's new tomb, which was near the place of execution. The women present noted the place of burial so that they could return at a later time and finish preparing the body.*

⤴ tomb, prepared, spices, fragrant oils

Draw Jesus in the tomb.

Pilate Set a Guard: *The chief priests and the Pharisees were worried that the disciples would steal Jesus' body. They asked Pilate for a guard to be set around His tomb, and he gave them their request. The chief priests sealed the stone entrance to the tomb and set a guard there.*

⤴ guard, seal

Draw the tomb entrance with a guard.

The Empty Tomb: *After the Sabbath, just at daybreak, the women came to Jesus' tomb in order to finish preparing His body for burial. Upon arriving they were greeted by an angel, who informed them that Jesus had risen from the dead and gave them instructions to tell the disciples.*

Draw an empty tomb.

Peter at the Tomb: *When the women returned and told the disciples that Jesus was not in the tomb, Peter and John ran to the tomb. Upon arriving they found it empty and the linen burial cloths folded up. The Peter left the tomb and marveled at what he had seen.*

⤴ handkerchief, linen cloths

Draw Peter looking into the empty tomb

2005

Grapevine Studies — New Testament — Lesson 24 — Level 1-2

THE BURIAL AND RESURRECTION

Bible Verses: Matthew 27:62–28:15; Luke 23:50-24:12; John 19:38-20:31
Time Frame: After the death of Jesus on the cross

Luke 23:50-56
John 19:38-42

Matt. 27:62-66

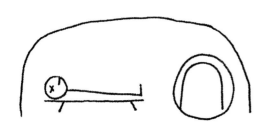
Jesus Was Buried

Pilate Set a Guard

Matt. 28:1-8
Luke 24:1-8

Luke 24:9-12
John 20:1-9

The Empty Tomb

Peter at the Tomb

SP 116

Grapevine Studies
New Testament

Lesson 24
Level 1-2

THE BURIAL AND RESURRECTION

Mary and Jesus: *Mary returned to the empty tomb to find two angels sitting where Jesus' body had been placed, and they asked why she was weeping. Mary responded that she wanted to know where the body had been removed to. Turning around, she encountered the risen Savior, who she at first mistook as the gardener.*

Draw Mary kneeling at Jesus' feet.

Jesus and the Disciples: *On Sunday evening ten of the disciples were gathered together, when Jesus appeared to them, showing them His nail-scarred hands and side. Jesus also gave them instructions during this visit.*

 peace   *Draw Jesus showing the disciples His hand.*

Jesus and Thomas: *The disciple Thomas, who was not present when Jesus appeared to the other disciples, questioned whether they had really seen Him. Eight days later, all eleven of the disciples were together, including Thomas, Jesus appeared again to them. This time Jesus showed Thomas His hands and His side and Thomas believed.*

Draw Jesus showing Thomas His hand.

The Conspiracy: *When the soldiers who had guarded Jesus' tomb returned with the report of the events that had taken place, the chief priests came up with a plan. The soldiers were told to say that the disciples had stolen the body of Jesus. In return the soldiers were given protection and paid to perpetuate this lie.*

Draw the chief priest paying a soldier.

1. Who buried Jesus? *Joseph of Arimathea and Nicodemus.*
2. Where was Jesus buried? *In Joseph of Arimathea's new tomb in a garden near the place of the crucifixion.*
3. Who requested that Pilate set a guard around Jesus' tomb? *The chief priests and Pharisees.*
4. What did the women find when they arrived at the tomb Sunday morning? *An empty tomb and an angel.*
5. What did Peter and John find when they arrived at the tomb? *An empty tomb and the burial clothes neatly folded.*
6. What did Mary find when she returned to the tomb? *An angel and then the risen Jesus.*
7. How did Jesus prove to His disciples who He was when He appeared to them? *By showing them His hands and side.*
8. What did the chief priests do when they found out Jesus had risen from the dead? *They paid the guards to spread the lie that Jesus' disciples had stolen his body.*
9. What do we learn about God from these verses? *Jesus did rise from the dead, proving His power over death and the grave.*

2005

Grapevine Studies
New Testament

Lesson 24
Level 1-2

John 20:11-16

Mary and Jesus

John 20:19-23

Jesus and Ten Disciples

John 20:24-31

Jesus and Thomas

Matt. 28:11-15

The Conspiracy

Lesson Review

1. Who buried Jesus?
2. Where was Jesus buried?
3. Who requested that Pilate set a guard around Jesus' tomb?
4. What did the women find when they arrived at the tomb Sunday morning?
5. What did Peter and John find when they arrived at the tomb?
6. What did Mary find when she returned to the tomb?
7. How did Jesus prove to His disciples who He was when He appeared to them?
8. What did the chief priests do when they found out Jesus had risen from the dead?
9. What do we learn about God from these verses?

Memory Verse: John 19:41-42

Review 4

1. Where did Jesus take His disciples to pray? *The Garden of Gethsemane.*
2. What did Jesus pray? *Not that His own will but would be done but that the will of the Father.*
3. Who strengthened Jesus in the garden? *An angel.*
4. What did the disciples do while Jesus prayed? *They slept.*
5. Who was included in the crowd that went to the garden to arrest Jesus? *Judas, the chief priests, officers of the temple and the elders.*
6. Who did Jesus heal? *The servant of the high priest.*
7. What did the disciples do when Jesus was arrested? *They fled.*
8. Recite Mark 14:36.
9. Who conducted the first trial of Jesus? *Annas.*
10. Who conducted the second trial of Jesus? *Caiaphas.*
11. What did Peter do when questioned about whether he was a disciple? *He denied it three times.*
12. What did the soldiers do to Jesus? *They beat and mocked him.*
13. Who conducted the third trial of Jesus? *Caiaphas and The Council/The Sanhedrin.*
14. What crime did The Council/Sanhedrin accuse Jesus of committing? *Blasphemy.*
15. What happened to Judas? *He hanged himself.*
16. Recite Matthew 26:57.
17. Who tried Jesus after the Sanhedrin? *Pontius Pilate.*
18. Why did Pilate send Jesus to Herod? *Jesus was from Herod's district.*
19. Who tried Jesus last? *Pontius Pilate.*
20. Who was Barabbas? *A criminal released by Pilate during the Feast of Passover.*
21. Why did Pilate wash his hands? *To make the statement that he was innocent in the death of Jesus.*
22. What did the soldiers do to Jesus? *They scourged Him, beat Him, put a scarlet/purple robe and a crown of thorns on Him, and then mocked Him.*
23. Recite Matthew 27:26.
24. Who carried the cross for Jesus? *Simon of Cyrene.*
25. What inscription did Pilate have put above Jesus? *Jesus of Nazareth, the King of the Jews.*
26. What happened to Jesus at Golgotha? *He was crucified.*
27. What did Jesus ask the Father to do to those who crucified Him? *Forgive those who crucified Him.*
28. Who cast lots for Jesus' tunic? *The soldiers who crucified Him.*
29. What did the crowd do to Jesus while He was on the cross? *They mocked Him.*

30. What did Jesus promise the repentant thief on the cross? *He would be with Jesus that day in Paradise.*
31. Recite Luke 23:33.
32. Whom did Jesus tell to take care of His mother? *The disciple whom He loved.*
33. What three things happened at the death of Jesus? *1) The temple veil was torn in two, 2) an earthquake struck, 3) the graves of the saints were opened and they appeared to many.*
34. Upon His death had Jesus completed the work given to Him by God the Father? *Yes.*
35. Who proclaimed at Jesus' death that He was the "Son of God"? *The centurion.*
36. Why did the soldier pierce Jesus' side? *To make sure He was dead.*
37. Recite Luke 23:46.
38. Who buried Jesus? *Joseph of Arimathea and Nicodemus.*
39. Where was Jesus buried? *In Joseph of Arimathea's new tomb, in a garden, near the place of the crucifixion.*
40. Who requested that Pilate set a guard around Jesus' tomb? *The chief priests and Pharisees.*
41. What did the women find when they arrived at the tomb Sunday morning? *An empty tomb and an angel.*
42. What did Peter and John find when they arrived at the tomb? *An empty tomb and the burial cloths neatly folded.*
43. What did Mary find when she returned to the tomb? *An angel and then the risen Jesus.*
44. How did Jesus prove to His disciples who He was when He appeared to them? *By showing them His hands and side.*
45. What did the chief priests do when they found out Jesus had risen from the dead? *They paid the guards to spread the lie that Jesus' disciples had stolen His body.*
46. Recite John 19:41-42.

Level 2

47. Name the books of the New Testament. *Matthew, Mark, Luke John, Acts, Romans, I & II Corinthians, Galatians, Ephesians, Philippians, Colossians, I & II Thessalonians, I & II Timothy, Titus, Philemon, Hebrews, James, I & II Peter, I, II & III John, Jude, and Revelation.*
48. Name The Twelve Apostles. *Andrew, Simon (Peter), Phillip, Matthew (Levi), James, John, Bartholomew, Thomas, James (son of Alphaeus), Lebbaeus, Simon (the Canaanite), and Judas Iscariot.*
49. Recite the first part of The Apostles Creed. *See page 307.*

Section 6 Goals and Key Points

THE ASCENSION

The goal of this lesson is learn about the events that took place between the resurrection and the ascension.

Key Points:
- After the resurrection, Jesus appeared to various people and groups of people for a period of forty days.
    - The two disciples who were traveling to Emmaus.
    - The apostles, on three different occasions.
    - As many as 500 at one time.
- Before His ascension Jesus gave His apostles final instructions to spread the gospel.
- Jesus ascended into the clouds and now sits at the right hand of the Father interceding for us.

WAS JESUS THE MESSIAH?

The goal of this lesson is to demonstrate that Jesus of Nazareth was the promised Messiah.

Key Points:
- Jesus was the Messiah, Hebrew for "the Anointed One."
- Jesus was the Christ, Greek for "the Anointed One."
- Jesus fulfilled all New Testament prophecies regarding the Messiah.
- The New Testament writers documented Jesus' life, death, and resurrection while many of the eyewitnesses to the events were alive.

THE HOLY SPIRIT

The goal of this lesson is to understand what took place at the giving of the Holy Spirit on the day of Pentecost.

Key Points:
- Before Jesus ascended, He commanded His apostles to go to Jerusalem and wait for the gift from the Father.
- While in the Jerusalem, the apostles, other disciples, and women, met in the upper room for prayer.
- The apostles replaced Judas with a man named Mathias.
- On the Feast of Pentecost, 50 days after the Feast of Passover, when the apostles, other disciples, and women were together in the upper room, the Holy Spirit was given.
- Once filled with the Holy Spirit, the apostles were able to preach in various languages to those gathered for Pentecost.

THE EARLY CHURCH

The goal of this lesson is to establish the facts surrounding the growth of the early Church.

Key Points:
- The early Church began in the upper Room on the day of Pentecost.
- Peter preached on Pentecost, and 3,000 men repented and were baptized.
- The early Church:
    1. Learned the apostles' doctrine.
    2. Fellowshipped together.
    3. Broke bread together.
    4. Prayed with one another.
    5. Gave to those in need.
    6. Worshipped in the temple.
    7. Added new believers were.

THE PERSECUTION

The goal of this lesson is to examine the events associated with the persecution of the early Church.

Key Points:
- Peter and John were arrested for healing a lame man in the name of Jesus. After being warned not to preach in Jesus' name, they were released.
- Peter and John continued to preach in Jesus' name.
- The apostles were arrested, but an angel released them from prison and they returned to preaching in Jesus' name.
- Stephen was first recorded martyr of Christianity.

Grapevine Studies
Old Testament

C/E Cards
Level 3

THE BURIAL AND RESURRECTION

Character/Event Cards

Create a card for the Burial and Resurrection.

> - *Jesus was buried by Joseph of Arimathea and Nicodemus.*
> - *Jesus was buried in a new tomb.*
> - *A guard was set at the tomb to insure that the disciples did not steal His body.*
> - *After three days Jesus rose from the grave.*
> - *Mary, Peter and the Disciples verified the resurrection by confirming that the tomb was empty.*

The Burial and Resurrection

Write your memory verse:

John 19:41-42

Level 2

Memory Work: Continue to memorize the Apostle's Creed.

2005

SP 120

Grapevine Studies — New Testament — Review Level 1-2

THE ASCENSION

Timeline Review

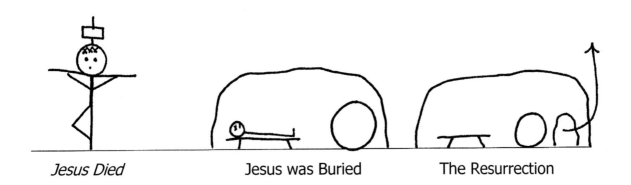

Jesus Died   Jesus was Buried   The Resurrection

Bible Verses

John 19:41-42

Luke 23:46

SP 121

Grapevine Studies
New Testament

Lesson 25
Level 1-2

THE ASCENSION

Background Bible Reading: Matthew 28; Mark 16; Luke 24; John 21; Acts 1
Time Frame: Forty days following the Resurrection

The Emmaus Road: *Two of Jesus' disciples (not apostles) were traveling to Emmaus and were discussing the events that had recently happened in Jerusalem. Jesus appeared and walked with them and expressed the desire to know what they were discussing. Jesus began explaining from the Scriptures all the things the prophets had said about the coming Messiah. The disciples did not know that it was Jesus who talked with them until they entered a town, sat down to eat, and Jesus broke bread with them. When they recognized Jesus, He left them. These disciples immediately returned to Jerusalem to tell the eleven apostles about what had happened.*

Draw Jesus talking to two men.   *Draw Jesus breaking bread and the two men.*

Jesus and His Disciples: *In obedience to Jesus' command (Matt. 28:7), the disciples went to Galilee. While waiting in Galilee, some the disciples decided to go fishing. After an unsuccessful night, Jesus greeted them and told them where to put down their nets. The catch was so large that the boat was threatening to capsize. At this point they realized it was Jesus and went ashore to meet Him.*

Draw Jesus near a fire with disciples running to meet Him and a net of fish.

Grapevine Studies
New Testament

Lesson 25
Level 1-2

THE ASCENSION

Bible Verses: Various
Time Frame: Forty days following the Resurrection

Luke 24:13-27

Luke 24:28-35

Mark 16:12-13

The Emmaus Road

John 21:1-14

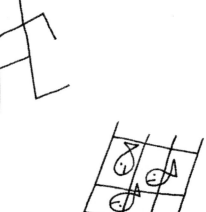

Jesus and His Disciples

2005

SP 122

Grapevine Studies
New Testament

Lesson 25
Level 1-2

THE ASCENSION

Jesus Appeared to Many: *After His resurrection, Jesus was seen by many people after His resurrection besides His disciples, and many of those who saw Him alive lived during the writing of what we call the New Testament.*

 Cephas   *Draw Jesus and a crowd.*

Final Instructions: *Before Jesus ascended to the Father, He gave some final instructions.*

disciples, baptizing, teaching, gospel   *Draw Jesus talking to His disciples.*

The Ascension: *At the end of forty days Jesus ascended into heaven to be seated at the right hand of the Father, where He now intercedes for us (Hebrews 8:25).*

Draw Jesus ascending a disciple watching.   *Draw God with Jesus at the right.*

1. What happened on the road to Emmaus? *Jesus appeared and talked with two disciples.*
2. Where were the disciples the third time Jesus appeared to them? *The Sea of Galilee/Tiberius.*
3. In addition to the Disciples, to whom did Jesus appear after His resurrection? *The two disciples on the road to Emmaus and to as many as 500 people at once.*
4. What were Jesus' final instructions to the disciples? *To go, preach the gospel, make disciples, baptize believers, and teach them to obey what He had taught them.*
5. What did Jesus do after appearing to His disciples and others for 40 days? *He ascended to the right hand of the Father.*
6. What do we learn about God from these verses? *God raised Jesus from the dead, and the proof of that was evident to the disciples and to the many people He appeared to after the resurrection.*

2005

Grapevine Studies
New Testament

Lesson 25
Level 1-2

I Cor. 15:3-7

Matt. 28:16-20

Mark 16:14-18

Jesus Appeared to Many

Final Instructions

Acts 1:1-11

Luke 24:50-53

Mark 16:19-20

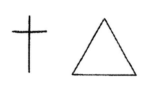

The Ascension

Lesson Review

1. What happened on the road to Emmaus?
2. Where were the disciples the third time Jesus appeared to them?
3. In addition to the disciples, to whom did Jesus appear to after His resurrection?
4. What were Jesus' final instructions to His disciples?
5. What did Jesus do after appearing to His disciples and others for forty days?
6. What do we learn about God from these verses?

Memory Verse: Mark 16:19

SP 123

Grapevine Studies
Old Testament

C/E Cards
Level 3

THE ASCENSION

Character/Event Cards

Create a card for the Ascension.

> - After the resurrection, Jesus made appearances over a period of 40 days.
>   1. The two disciples on the road to Emmaus.
>   2. The Apostles
>   3. As many as 500 people at one time.
>
> - Before His ascension Jesus gave His Apostles final instructions, to spread the gospel.
> - Jesus ascended into the clouds and now sits at the right hand of the Father interceding for us

The Ascension

Write your memory verse:

Mark 16:19

Level 2

Memory Work: Continue to memorize the Apostle's Creed.

2005

SP 124

Grapevine Studies
New Testament

Review
Level 1-2

WAS JESUS THE MESSIAH?

Timeline Review

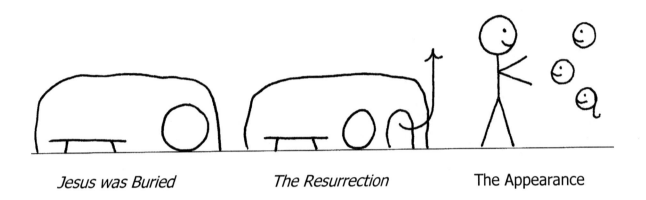

Jesus was Buried The Resurrection The Appearance

Bible Verses

Mark 16:19

John 19:41-42

2005

SP 125

Grapevine Studies
New Testament

Lesson 26
Level 1-2

WAS JESUS THE MESSIAH? (Part 1)

Background Bible Reading: Study Messianic Prophecies
Time Frame: Throughout History

Messiah: *See notes on page opposing page.*

Christ: *See notes on page opposing page.*

Genealogy of Jesus: *Two of the gospel writers mention the genealogy of Jesus: Matthew and Luke. Matthew follows Joseph's line, sometimes called the "royal lineage," and Luke follows the line of Mary, sometimes called the "common lineage." Although Joseph was not Jesus' biological father, the author of Matthew deemed his genealogy to be important. Between Adam and Jesus there were sixty-two generations.*

generations
2005

Fill in the blanks.

Grapevine Studies
New Testament

Lesson 26
Level 1-2

WAS JESUS THE MESSIAH?

Bible Verses: Various
Time Frame: Throughout History

Messiah: *Hebrew* for "Anointed One"

Christ: *Greek* for "Anointed One"

| Matt. 1:1-17 | Genealogy of Jesus | Luke 3:23-38 |

Line of *Joseph*   Line of *Mary*

Adam

10 Generations

Noah

10 Generations

Abraham

14 Generations

David

14 Generations

Captivity in Babylon

14 Generations

Jesus

2005

SP 126

Grapevine Studies
New Testament

Lesson 26
Level 1-2

WAS JESUS THE MESSIAH? (Part 1)

This lesson, and the one following, is designed to give a sampling of the prophecies fulfilled by Jesus of Nazareth. It is my desire as the author to show clearly that Jesus of Nazareth was and is the long-awaited Jewish Messiah.

Fill in the blanks.

1. What is the Hebrew term for "Anointed One"? *Messiah.*
2. What is the Greek term for "Anointed One"? *Christ.*
3. Name three Messianic prophecies fulfilled by Jesus of Nazareth. *See lesson.*

2005

Grapevine Studies
New Testament

Lesson 26
Level 1-2

New Testament Prophecy		New Testament Fulfillment
Genesis 3:15	Born of *woman*	Matthew 1:18
		Galatians 4:4
Micah 5:2	Born in *Bethlehem*	Luke 2:4-7
Hosea 11:1	Out of *Egypt* Messiah would come	Matthew 2:13-15
Jeremiah 31:15	*Death* of the children	Matthew 2:16-18
Judges 13:5	From *Nazareth* Called a *Nazarene*	Matthew 2:21-23
Isaiah 40:3	One would go before and *prepare the way* for Messiah	John 1:6-7, 19-23

Lesson Review

1. What is the Hebrew term for "Anointed One"?
2. What is the Greek term for "Anointed One"?
3. Name three Messianic prophecies fulfilled by Jesus of Nazareth.

Memory Verse: John 1:14

2005

SP 127

Grapevine Studies
Old Testament

C/E Cards
Level 3

WAS JESUS THE MESSIAH?

Character/Event Cards

Create a card for Jesus the Messiah.

> - *Jesus was the Messiah, Hebrew for the Anointed One.*
> - *Jesus was the Christ, Greek for the Anointed One.*
> - *Jesus fulfilled all Old Testament prophecies regarding the Messiah.*
> - *The New Testament writers documented Jesus' life, death and resurrection while many of the eye witnesses to the events were still living.*

Jesus the Messiah

Write your memory verse:

John 1:14

Level 2

Memory Work: Continue to memorize the Apostle's Creed.

2005

SP 128

WAS JESUS THE MESSIAH?

Timeline Review

Jesus was Buried   The Resurrection   The Appearance

Bible Verses

John 1:14

Mark 16:19

Grapevine Studies
New Testament

Lesson 27
Level 1-2

WAS JESUS THE MESSIAH? (Part 2)

Background Bible Reading: Study Messianic Prophecies
Time Frame: Throughout History

Messiah: *See notes on page opposing page.*

Christ: *See notes on page opposing page.*

This lesson, and the one following, is designed to give a sampling of the prophecies fulfilled by Jesus of Nazareth. It is my desire as the author to show clearly that Jesus of Nazareth was and is the long-awaited Jewish Messiah.

Fill in the blanks

Grapevine Studies
New Testament

Lesson 27
Level 1-2

WAS JESUS THE MESSIAH?

Bible Verses: Various
Time Frame: Throughout History

Messiah: *Hebrew* for "Anointed One."

Christ: *Greek* for "Anointed One."

New Testament Prophecy		New Testament Fulfillment
Isaiah 42:1-4, 53:4	Healed the *sick*	Matthew 8:15-17
Zechariah 9:9	Messiah will come on a *donkey*	Matthew 21:6-9
Psalm 118:22-23	Messiah will be *rejected*	Matthew 21:42-46
Zechariah 13:7 Daniel 9:26	Shepherd will be *struck* Sheep will be *scattered*	Matthew 26:56 Mark 14:50
Psalm 27:12	*Falsely* accused	Matthew 26:60
Isaiah 53:7	*Silent* when accused	Matthew 26:62-63

SP 130

Grapevine Studies
New Testament

Lesson 27
Level 1-2

WAS JESUS THE MESSIAH? (Part 2)

This lesson, and the one following, is designed to give a sampling of the prophecies fulfilled by Jesus of Nazareth. It is my desire as the author to show clearly that Jesus of Nazareth was and is the long-awaited Jewish Messiah.

Fill in the blanks

What is the Hebrew term for "Anointed One"? *Messiah.*

What is the Greek term for "Anointed One"? *Christ.*

Name three Messianic prophecies that Jesus of Nazareth fulfilled. *See lesson.*

Grapevine Studies
New Testament
Lesson 27
Level 1-2

New Testament Prophecy / New Testament Fulfillment

New Testament Prophecy		New Testament Fulfillment
Psalm 22:18	Messiah's garment *divided*	Luke 23:34
Isaiah 53:12	Numbered among *transgressors*	Luke 23:32-33
Psalm 34:20	None of Messiah's bones will be *broken*	John 19:33
Psalm 22:16	Messiah will be *pierced*	John 19:34
Isaiah 53:9	Buried with the *wicked*	Matthew 27:57-60

If Jesus is Messiah, what should be our response?

Lesson Review

1. What is the Hebrew term for "Anointed One"?
2. What is the Greek term for "Anointed One"?
3. Name three Messianic prophecies fulfilled by Jesus of Nazareth.

Memory Verse: John 20:30-31

2005

SP 131

Grapevine Studies
Old Testament

C/E Cards
Level 3

WAS JESUS THE MESSIAH?

Character/Event Cards

Continue to add to the card for Jesus the Messiah.

> - *Record Prophecies and fulfillments that you deem important for your students to remember.*

Jesus the Messiah

Write your memory verse:

John 20:30-31

Level 2

Memory Work: Continue to memorize the Apostle's Creed.

2005

SP 132

Grapevine Studies
New Testament

Review
Level 1-2

THE HOLY SPIRIT

Timeline Review

Jesus was Buried   The Resurrection   The Appearance

Bible Verses

John 20:30-31

John 1:14

2005

SP 133

Grapevine Studies
New Testament

Lesson 28
Level 1-2

THE HOLY SPIRIT

Background Bible Reading: Acts 1-2
Time Frame: Fifty days after the Resurrection

The Command: *Before Jesus ascended into heaven, He commanded the apostles to wait in Jerusalem until they received the promise from the Father. After they received this promise, they would be His witnesses throughout all the earth.*

 promise, baptize   *Draw Jesus issuing instructions.*

The Upper Room: *In obedience to Jesus' command, the apostles, the women, Jesus' mother and brothers returned to Jerusalem and gathered in the upper room to pray.*

Draw two people praying.

Choosing a New Apostle: *While in Jerusalem awaiting the promise of God, the apostles decided to replace Judas. The qualifications for the new apostle would be a man who had been with them from the time of Jesus' baptism and had been a witness of His resurrection.*

Draw Jesus' baptism with an arrow pointing to the resurrection.

Matthias: *The apostles drew lots between two men, and Matthias, to become one of the twelve apostles.*

 lots   *Draw Matthias.*

2005

Grapevine Studies
New Testament

Lesson 28
Level 1-2

THE HOLY SPIRIT

Bible Verses: Acts 1:1-2:12
Time Frame: Fifty days after the Resurrection

Acts 1:1-11

The Command

Acts 1:12-14

The Upper Room

Acts 1:15-22

Choosing a New Apostle

Acts 1:23-26

Matthias

2005

SP 134

Grapevine Studies
New Testament

Lesson 28
Level 1-2

THE HOLY SPIRIT

The Holy Spirit: *On the day of Pentecost (Lev. 23:15-22 Feast of Pentecost/Weeks), when they (apostles, disciples, and the women) were in the upper room and all in one accord, they were filled with the Holy Spirit and spoke in other tongues as the Spirit enabled them.*

👆 one accord, tongues, filled   *Draw people worshipping/praying and tongues above them.*

Preaching: *The apostles began to preach in the native languages of those gathered in Jerusalem from all over the known world to celebrate the Feast of Pentecost/Weeks.*

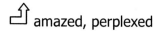 devout   *Draw an apostle preaching to a group of Jewish men.*

The Crowd: *When these men heard the apostles preaching in their native languages, they marveled and asked what this meant.*

👆 amazed, perplexed   *Draw two men talking to one another.*

1. Where did Jesus tell the apostles to stay? *Jerusalem.*
2. How long were the disciples to stay in Jerusalem? *Until they received the gift from the Father.*
3. What were the qualifications for the apostle who replaced Judas? *He had to be a witness of Jesus' baptism and His resurrection.*
4. Who was chosen as the new apostle? *Matthias.*
5. What happened in the upper room on the day of Pentecost? *The Holy Spirit came upon the people in the room in the form of tongues of fire.*
6. What did the apostles do after the Holy Spirit was given to them? *They preached to those in Jerusalem.*
7. How did the crowds respond to hearing the apostles preach in their languages? *They were amazed and asked what it meant.*
8. What do we learn about God from these verses? *When the Holy Spirit was given, He indwelt and empowered the apostles to fulfill what Jesus had commissioned them to do.*

2005

Grapevine Studies
New Testament

Lesson 28
Level 1-2

Acts 2:1-4

The Holy Spirit

Acts 2:5-8

Acts 2:9-12

Preaching

The Crowd

Lesson Review

1. Where did Jesus tell the apostles to stay?
2. How long were the disciples to stay in Jerusalem?
3. What were the qualifications for the apostle who replaced Judas?
4. Who was chosen as the new apostle?
5. What happened in the upper room on the day of Pentecost?
6. What did the apostles do after the Holy Spirit was given to them?
7. How did the crowds respond to hearing the apostles preach in their languages?
8. What do we learn about God from these verses?

Memory Verse: Acts 1:8

2005

SP 135

Grapevine Studies
Old Testament

C/E Cards
Level 3

THE HOLY SPIRIT

Character/Event Cards

Create a card for the Holy Spirit.

> - *Jesus commanded the Apostles to go to Jerusalem where they would receive a gift from the Father.*
> - *The Apostles, woman and other disciples prayed in the Upper Room.*
> - *On Pentecost, the Holy Spirit came on all those in the Upper Room.*
> - *After being filled with the Holy Spirit the Apostles preached to those in Jerusalem, in their own native languages.*

The Holy Spirit

Write your memory verse:

Acts 1:8

Level 2

Memory Work: Continue to memorize the Apostle's Creed.

2005

SP 136

THE EARLY CHURCH

Timeline Review

The Appearance   The Ascension   The Holy Spirit

Bible Verses

Acts 1:8

John 20:30-31

Grapevine Studies
New Testament

Lesson 29
Level 1-2

THE EARLY CHURCH

Background Bible Reading: Acts 1-2
Time Frame: After the Holy Spirit was given to the Church

Peter Preached: *On the day of Pentecost, after the Holy Spirit had filled the believers in the upper room, the apostles began to preach to the men in Jerusalem. Peter stood up and reminded the men present of the promises of the New Testament concerning the Christ and revealed that Jesus was the Christ.*

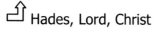 Hades, Lord, Christ   *Draw Peter preaching.*

The Response: *When the men in Jerusalem heard Peter's message, they asked what they should do. Peter responded by calling them to repent, and be baptized in the name of Jesus Christ, and as a result they would receive the Holy Spirit.*

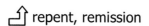 repent, remission   *Draw the men repenting.*

The Baptisms: *After hearing Peter's message, many of the men of Jerusalem repented, and that day 3,000 of them were baptized.*

baptized   *Draw a man being baptized.*

2005

Grapevine Studies
New Testament

Lesson 29
Level 1-2

THE EARLY CHURCH

Bible Verses: Acts 2:5-47
Time Frame: After the Holy Spirit was given to the Church

Acts 2:5-8, 12-36

Peter Preached

Acts 2:37-40

Acts 2:41

The Response

The Baptisms

SP 138

Grapevine Studies
New Testament

Lesson 29
Level 1-2

THE EARLY CHURCH

The Early Church: The early Church was marked by the following practices:

1. Continued in the apostles' doctrine

⇧ doctrine   *Draw a man teaching.*

2. Fellowship

⇧ fellowship   *Draw two people talking.*

3. Broke bread together

⇧ broke bread   *Draw a loaf of bread broken.*

4. Prayed

⇧ prayers, fear   *Draw two people praying together.*

5. Gave to and shared with one another

Draw a person handing another person something.

6. Worshipped daily at the temple

Draw a man worshipping at the temple.

7. New believers were added

⇧ saved   *Draw people smiling.*

---

1. Who stood up and preached to the men in Jerusalem at Pentecost? *Peter and the apostles.*
2. How did the men of Jerusalem respond to Peter's preaching? *They were "cut to the heart" and wanted to know what they should do.*
3. How many were baptized as a result of Peter's preaching? *3,000.*
4. What are some things that marked the early Church? *They continued in the Apostles' doctrine, fellowship, breaking of bread, prayer, giving, and worship, and new believers were added to the Church every day.*
5. What do we learn about God from these verses? *God changes men's lives through the Word and through believers.*

2005

Grapevine Studies
New Testament

Lesson 29
Level 1-2

Acts 2:42-47

The Early Church

1. Continued in the apostle's doctrine.

2. Fellowship.

3. Broke bread together.

4. Prayed.

5. Gave to and shared with one another.

6. Worshipped daily at the temple.

7. New believers were added.

Lesson Review

1. Who stood up and preached to the men in Jerusalem at Pentecost?
2. How did the men of Jerusalem respond to Peter's preaching?
3. How many were baptized as a result of Peter's preaching?
4. What are some things that marked the early Church?
5. What do we learn about God from these verses?

Memory Verse: Acts 2:42

2005

SP 139

Grapevine Studies
Old Testament

C/E Cards
Level 3

THE EARLY CHURCH

Character/Event Cards

Create a card for the Early Church.

> - *The Church began on the day of Pentecost when the Holy Spirit was given to believers in the Upper Room.*
> - *The Early Church:*
>   1. *Learned the Apostles doctrine.*
>   2. *Fellowshipped.*
>   3. *Broke bread together.*
>   4. *Prayed for one another.*
>   5. *Gave to those in need.*
>   6. *Worshipped in Temple.*
>   7. *New believers were added.*

The Early Church

Write your memory verse:

Acts 2:42

Level 2

Memory Work: Continue to memorize the Apostle's Creed.

2005

SP 140

THE PERSECUTION

Timeline Review

The Ascension   The Holy Spirit   The Early Church

Bible Verses

Acts 2:42

Acts 1:8

Grapevine Studies
New Testament

Lesson 30
Level 1-2

THE PERSECUTION

Background Bible Reading: Acts 3-7
Time Frame: The early Church

The Lame Man Was Healed: *One day, as Peter and John went to the temple at the hour of prayer, they encountered a man lame from birth. Instead of giving him alms, they healed they healed in the name of Jesus Christ. The man then went into the temple leaping and praising God.*

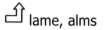 lame, alms   *Draw a man leaping.*

Peter Preached: *When the people saw the lame man healed, they were amazed. Peter then took the opportunity to tell the people about Jesus and how faith in Jesus had healed the lame man.*

Draw Peter preaching to men.

Peter and John Were Arrested: *After the priests, Sadducees, and the captain of the temple heard the sermon Peter had preached, they had Peter and John arrested because they spoke of the resurrection of Jesus. When Peter and John were questioned by the religious leaders of that day, the leaders were amazed with their answers because Peter and John were unlearned men. The religious leaders also remembered that these men had been with Jesus.*

 Sadducees   *Draw Peter and John in chains.*

Peter and John Were Released: *When the religious leaders realized there was no justification for punishing Peter and John, they commanded them not to speak or teach in the name of Jesus. Peter and John stated that they must obey God rather than men. After their release they went to their companions and prayed for courage, boldness, and opportunity.*

Draw Peter and John praying and the Holy Spirit over them.

THE PERSECUTION

Bible Verses: Acts 3:1-7:60
Time Frame: The early Church

Acts 3:1-8

Acts 3:9-16

The Lame Man Was Healed

Peter Preached

Acts 4:1-14

Acts 4:18-31

Peter and Were John Arrested

Peter and John Were Released

THE PERSECUTION

The Apostles Were Arrested: *The apostles continued to preach the gospel, heal the sick, and perform miracles, which led the religious leaders to put them in prison.*

 esteemed   *Draw the apostles arrested.*

The Angel: *That night, an angel of the Lord went to the prison where the apostles were being held and released them. The angel told them to return to the temple and teach the people.*

Draw an angel opening a door.

Stephen Was Tried: *Stephen was great in faith and was being used of God. Stephen's enemies falsely accused him and had him arrested. When he was on trial he gave a speech showing that Jesus was the Christ. Stephen then pointed out the sins of the religious leaders, which made them very angry.*

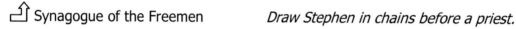 Synagogue of the Freemen   *Draw Stephen in chains before a priest.*

Stephen Was Stoned: *After Stephen's speech, the religious leaders stoned Stephen to death.*

 stoned   *Draw Stephen dead.*

1. Who was healed when Peter and John went to the temple? *A man lame from birth.*
2. How many believed when Peter preached following the healing of the lame man? *5,000.*
3. What command did the religious leaders give Peter and John when they were released? *Not to speak or teach in Jesus' name.*
4. When the apostles were arrested, how were they released from prison? *An angel of the Lord released them.*
5. How did Stephen respond to the accusations against him? *He reminded the religious leaders of the prophecies concerning the Messiah and then pointed out their failure to recognize that these prophecies had been fulfilled in Jesus.*
6. What happened to Stephen? *He was falsely accused and stoned to death.*
7. What do we learn about God from these verses? *God takes care of His people, whether it is in life or in death.*

Grapevine Studies
New Testament

Lesson 30
Level 1-2

Acts 5:12-18

Acts 5:19-20

The Apostles Were Arrested

The Angel

Acts 6:8-15; 7:1-2, 51-54

Acts 7:55-60

Stephen Was Tried

Stephen Was Stoned

Lesson Review

1. Who was healed when Peter and John went to the temple?
2. How many believed when Peter preached following the healing of the lame man?
3. What command did the religious leaders give Peter and John when they were released?
4. When the apostles were arrested, how were they released from prison?
5. How did Stephen respond to the accusations against him?
6. What happened to Stephen?
7. What do we learn about God from these verses?

Memory Verse: Acts 7:59

2005

SP 143

Grapevine Studies
New Testament

Review 5
Level 1-2

Review 5

1. What happened on the road to Emmaus? *Jesus appeared and talked with two disciples.*
2. Where were the disciples the third time Jesus appeared to them? *The Sea of Galilee/Tiberius.*
3. In addition to the disciples, to whom did Jesus appear after His resurrection? *The two disciples on the road to Emmaus and to as many as 500 people at once.*
4. What were Jesus' final instructions to the disciples? *To go, preach the gospel, make disciples, baptize believers, and teach them to obey what He had taught them.*
5. What did Jesus do after appearing to His disciples and others for forty days? *He ascended to the Father.*
6. Recite Mark 16:19.
7. What is the Hebrew term for "Anointed One"? *Messiah.*
8. What is the Greek term for "Anointed One"? *Christ.*
9. Name six Messianic prophecies fulfilled by Jesus of Nazareth. *See lesson.*
10. Recite John 1:14.
11. Recite John 20:30-31.
12. Where did Jesus tell the apostles to stay? *Jerusalem.*
13. How long were the disciples to stay in Jerusalem? *Until they received the gift from the Father.*
14. What were the qualifications for the apostle who replaced Judas? *He had to be a witness of Jesus' baptism and His resurrection.*
15. Who was chosen as the new apostle? *Matthias.*
16. What happened in the upper room on the day of Pentecost? *The Holy Spirit came upon the people in the room.*
17. What did the apostles do after the Holy Spirit was given to them? *They preached to those in Jerusalem.*
18. How did the crowds respond to hearing the apostles preach in their languages? *They were amazed and asked what it meant.*

Grapevine Studies
New Testament
Review 5
Level 1-2

19. Recite Acts 1:8.
20. Who stood up and preached to the men in Jerusalem on Pentecost? *Peter and the apostles.*
21. How did the men of Jerusalem respond to Peter's preaching? *They were "cut to the heart" and wanted to know what they should do.*
22. How many were baptized as a result of Peter's preaching? *3,000.*
23. What are some things that marked the early Church? *They continued in the Apostles' doctrine, fellowship, breaking of bread, prayer, giving, worship, and new believers to the Church daily.*
24. Recite Acts 2:42.
25. Who was healed when Peter and John went to the temple? *A man lame from birth.*
26. How many believed when Peter preached following the healing of the lame man? *5,000.*
27. What command did the religious leaders give Peter and John when they were released? *Not to speak or teach in Jesus' name.*
28. When the apostles were arrested, how were they released from prison? *An angel of the Lord released them.*
29. How did Stephen respond to the accusations against him? *He reminded the religious leaders of the prophecies concerning the Messiah and then pointed out their failure to recognize that these prophecies had been fulfilled in Jesus.*
30. What happened to Stephen? *He was falsely accused and stoned to death.*
31. Recite Acts 7:59.

Level 2

32. Name the books of the New Testament. *Matthew, Mark, Luke John, Acts, Romans, I & II Corinthians, Galatians, Ephesians, Philippians, Colossians, I & II Thessalonians, I & II Timothy, Titus, Philemon, Hebrews, James, I & II Peter, I, II & III John, Jude, and Revelation.*
33. Name The Twelve Apostles. *Andrew, Simon (Peter), Phillip, Matthew (Levi), James, John, Bartholomew, Thomas, James (son of Alphaeus), Lebbaeus, Simon (the Canaanite), and Judas Iscariot.*
34. Recite the first half of The Apostles Creed. *See page 307.*

Grapevine Studies
New Testament

Section 7
Level 1-2

Section 7 Goals and Key Points

SAUL

The goal of this lesson is introduce students to the man Paul.

Key Points:

- Saul was present at the stoning of Stephen.
- Saul was a persecutor of the early Church.
- Jesus appeared to Saul on the road to Damascus, and from that point on Saul believed that Jesus was the Messiah.

PAUL

The goal of this lesson is introduce students to the man Paul.

Key Points:

- Saul and Paul are the same man.
- Paul's mission in life was to preach the Gospel to the Gentiles, the Jews, and kings.
- Paul wrote many of the New Testament epistles.

LETTERS TO THE CHURCHES

The goal of this lesson is to look briefly at the New Testament epistles.

Key Points:

- The New Testament epistles/letters were written to Churches and individuals.
- The epistles were meant to correct, encourage, exhort, and teach.
- There are twenty-two New Testament epistles.
- Paul wrote thirteen of the epistles.

2005

THE GOSPEL IN STICK FIGURING

The goal of this lesson is to show how the Gospel can be taught with stick figures and Scripture.

Key Points:
- The main points of the Gospel are:
    1. Creation
    2. Sin
    3. The Promise
    4. The Messiah
    5. Sinless Life
    6. Died
    7. Buried
    8. Rose
    9. Ascended
    10. Restored
    11. Coming Again
    12. Judgment

SHARING THE GOSPEL

The goal of this lesson is to learn a simple method for sharing the Gospel and to learn ways that believers can grow in their faith.

Key Points:
- The main points of understanding the Gospel are:
    1. I am a sinner.
    2. Jesus died for me.
    3. I need to repent.
    4. I can receive God's forgiveness.

- I can grow in my faith by:
    1. Leaning and obeying the Bible.
    2. Fellowshipping with other believers.
    3. Praying.
    4. Celebrating communion.
    5. Being baptized.
    6. Sharing the Gospel.

Grapevine Studies
Old Testament

C/E Cards
Level 3

THE PERSECUTION

Character/Event Cards

Create a card for the Persecution.

> - *Peter and John were arrested for healing a lame man in the name of Jesus. After warning Peter and John not to preach in Jesus' name they were released.*
> - *Peter and John continued to preach in Jesus' name.*
> - *The Apostles were arrested but an angel released them from prison and they returned to preaching in Jesus' name.*
> - *Stephen was first recorded martyr of Christianity.*

The Persecution

Write your memory verse:

Acts 7:59

Level 2

Memory Work: Continue to memorize the Apostle's Creed. *If your students have memorized the Apostle's Creed, an optional activity is to have them stick figure the various phrases of the creed.*

2005

SP 146

SAUL

Timeline Review

The Holy Spirit *The Early Church* The Persecution

Bible Verses

Acts 7:59

Acts 2:42

Grapevine Studies
New Testament

Lesson 31
Level 1-2

SAUL

Background Bible Reading: Acts 7-11
Time Frame: The early Church

Saul at Stephen's Death: *Saul was present at the stoning of Stephen.*

Draw Saul with coats at his feet.

Saul Persecuted the Church: *The death of Stephen marked an escalation in the persecution of the Church. Saul joined in actively persecuting the Church, which caused the believers to scatter throughout the area. They preached the Gospel wherever they went.*

Draw a man running then that man preaching.

The Road to Damascus: *Saul's pursuit of those following the Way led him to seek believers living in Damascus. After obtaining letters to take to the synagogues there, Saul began a journey that would forever change his life. On the road to Damascus, the Lord Jesus Christ appeared to Saul and convicted him of wrongdoing. This appearance by Jesus to Saul convinced Saul that Jesus was the Messiah and it was futile to keep resisting Him. The appearance left Saul blind so that he had to be led into Damascus by his traveling companions.*

 The Way   *Draw Saul kneeling and a light coming from heaven.*

Ananias: *After entering Damascus, Saul fasted for three days. The Lord appeared to Ananias and told him to go and pray for Saul. Ananias had heard the reports about Saul persecuting the Church, but the Lord assured him that Saul was indeed chosen by God for a special assignment.*

Draw the Lord speaking to Ananias.

Grapevine Studies
New Testament

Lesson 31
Level 1-2

SAUL

Bible Verses: Acts 7:57-11:26
Time Frame: The early Church

Acts 7:57-60

Acts 8:1-4

Saul at Stephen's Death

Saul Persecuted the Church

Acts 9:1-8

Acts 9:9-16

The Road to Damascus

Ananias

SP 148

Grapevine Studies
New Testament

Lesson 31
Level 1-2

SAUL

Saul Was Baptized: *Ananias prayed for Saul. Saul received his sight and was baptized. Saul then remained in Damascus with the disciples there.*

Draw Ananias praying for Saul.

Saul Preached: *After Saul was baptized, he immediately began to preach that Jesus was the Christ to the Jews in the synagogue. The Jews were amazed by what he said and could not disprove what Saul said in regard to Jesus being the Messiah. The Jews then sought to kill Saul, but the disciples helped him to escape the city.*

Draw Saul in a basket hanging over a wall.

Saul and the Apostles: *Saul returned from Damascus to Jerusalem, where he attempted to unite with the believers there. The disciples were skeptical of his conversion, but a disciple named Barnabas took Saul to the apostles. Saul told the apostles of his conversion and he remained in Jerusalem preaching among the Jews. Again the Jews attempted to kill Saul, but, the plan was discovered and Saul was sent to Tarsus.*

 Hellenists   *Draw Saul talking to the apostles.*

Saul and Barnabas: *When the Church was scattered by persecution after the death of Stephen, some of the believers settled in Antioch. These believers preached the Gospel, and many people believed. When word of these believers reached Jerusalem, Barnabas and Saul were chosen to go to Antioch and verify the account. Barnabas and Saul remained in Antioch for a year, teaching the disciples there.*

Christians   *Draw a man teaching.*

1. What happened to the Church after Stephen was stoned? *The Church entered a time of persecution, which caused the believers to scatter and preach the gospel into new areas.*
2. What role did Saul play in the persecution of the Church? *Saul was one of the main persecutors of the early Church.*
3. What happened to Saul on the road to Damascus? *The Lord appeared to Saul, and he was struck blind and believed that Jesus was the Messiah.*
4. Who was Ananias? *A believer from Damascus, whom the Lord spoke and who prayed for Saul to receive his sight.*
5. How did Saul leave Damascus? *In a basket, let down over the city wall.*
6. When Saul returned to Jerusalem, how was he received by the disciples, Barnabas, and the Apostles? *The disciples doubted his conversion, while Barnabas and the apostles believed that Saul had truly become a believer.*
7. Why did Barnabas and Saul go to Antioch, and what did they do there? *They went to verify the fact that many Jews had become believers there, and they stayed to teach the people.*
8. What do we learn about God from these verses? *God can use persecution to move believers and to spread the Gospel.*

2005

Grapevine Studies
New Testament

Lesson 31
Level 1-2

Acts 9:17-19

Acts 9:20-25

Saul Was Baptized

Saul Preached

Acts 9:26-30

Acts 11:19-26

Saul and the Apostles

Saul and Barnabas

Lesson Review

1. What happened to the Church after Stephen was stoned?
2. What role did Saul play in the persecution of the Church?
3. What happened to Saul on the road to Damascus?
4. Who was Ananias?
5. How did Saul leave Damascus?
6. When Saul returned to Jerusalem, how was he received by the disciples, Barnabas, and the apostles?
7. Why did Barnabas and Saul go to Antioch, and what did they do there?
8. What do we learn about God from these verses?

Memory Verse: Acts 9:15-16

Grapevine Studies
Old Testament

C/E Cards
Level 3

SAUL

Character/Event Cards

Create a card for Saul.

- *Saul was present at the stoning of Stephen.*
- *Saul was a persecutor of the early Church.*
- *Jesus appeared to Saul on the road to Damascus and from that point on Saul believed that Jesus was the Messiah.*

Saul

Write your memory verse:

Acts 9:15-16

Level 2

Memory Work: Continue to memorize the Apostle's Creed.

2005

SP 150

Grapevine Studies — New Testament — Review — Level 1-2

PAUL

Timeline Review

The Holy Spirit · The Early Church · The Persecution

Bible Verses

Acts 9:15-16

Acts 7:59

Acts 2:42

2005

SP 151

Grapevine Studies
New Testament
Lesson 32
Level 1-2

PAUL

Background Bible Reading: Acts 9, 13, 18, 26; I Corinthians 11; II Timothy 4
Time Frame: The early Church

Paul's Mission: *When God spoke to Ananias regarding Paul, the Lord told him that Paul would bear His name to the Gentiles, to kings, and to the Jews. God also said Paul would suffer for His name.*

 Gentile *Write Jews, Kings, Gentiles, Sufferings.*

Saul and Paul: *At this time in history it was not uncommon to be known by two names. Saul was possibly the Hebrew name while Paul was the Roman version.*

Write Saul = Paul.

Paul Preached to the Gentiles: *Upon leaving the synagogue in Antioch, Paul and Barnabas were approached by Gentiles, who requested that they preach to them the following Sabbath. When Paul preached to the Gentiles, some of the Jews were filled with envy and opposed Paul, but the Gentiles received the Word with gladness and glorified the Lord.*

Draw two men, one labeled a Jew and one a Gentile.

Paul Preached to the Jews: *As Paul went out to preach the Gospel: he would spend his Sabbaths in synagogues reasoning with the Jews of that town. While he was in Corinth, some of the Jews opposed Paul, but many believed, including the ruler of the synagogue.*

tentmakers, reasoned   *Draw Paul reasoning in the "synagogue."*

2005

Grapevine Studies
New Testament

Lesson 32
Level 1-2

PAUL

Bible Verses: Various
Time Frame: The early Church

Acts 9:15

Acts 13:9

Jews

Kings

Gentiles

Suffering

Saul = Paul

Paul's Mission

Saul and Paul

Acts 13:42-49

Acts 18:1-11

Paul Preached to the Gentiles

Paul Preached to the Jews

SP 152

2005

Grapevine Studies
New Testament

Lesson 32
Level 1-2

Paul

Paul Preached to a King: *While in Caesarea, had an opportunity to testify before King Agrippa, who was king of the northern part of Israel. King Agrippa responded that Paul had almost persuaded him to become a Christian.*

👆 persuaded   *Draw Paul talking to a king.*

Sufferings of Paul: *Just as the Lord had said, Paul suffered many things for the name of Jesus Christ. His sufferings included being stoned, beaten, and shipwrecked.*

Draw Saul being stoned or beaten.

Books Written by Paul: *As Paul traveled, he often began Churches in the cities where he stayed. Paul would later write letters to these Churches to encourage, exhort, correct, and teach them the ways of the Lord. Paul also wrote letters to individuals, including Philemon, Timothy, and Titus. (We will identify Paul's letters in the next two lessons.)*

Draw a letter.

Paul View of His Death: *As Paul wrote his last letter before his death, he told Timothy that he had done what the Lord had called him to do and that he looked forward to his crown of righteousness.*

👆 crown, righteousness   *Draw a man running toward a crown.*

1. What was Paul's mission from God? *To preach the Gospel to the Gentiles, to kings, and to the Jews.*
2. What other name was Paul known by? *Saul.*
3. What was the response of the Gentiles when Paul preached? *Many received the Word with gladness and glorified the Lord.*
4. What was the response of King Agrippa to Paul's preaching? *He was almost persuaded.*
5. What was the response of the Jews to Paul's preaching? *Some opposed but some believed, including the ruler of the synagogue.*
6. Name some of the things Paul suffered for the name of Jesus. *Stoning, shipwreck, and beatings.*
7. What was Paul's view of his death? *He looked forward to the crown of righteousness.*
8. What do we learn about God from these verses? *God desires that all Gentiles, kings, and Jews come to believe.*

2005

Grapevine Studies
New Testament

Lesson 32
Level 1-2

Acts 26:27-29

Paul Preached to a King

II Cor. 11:22-28

Sufferings of Paul

II Tim. 4:6-8

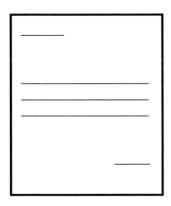

Books Written by Paul

Paul's View of His Death

Lesson Review

1. What was Paul's mission from God?
2. What other name was Paul known by?
3. What was the response of the Gentiles when Paul preached?
4. What was the response of King Agrippa to Paul's preaching?
5. What was the response of the Jews to Paul's preaching?
6. Name some of the things Paul suffered for the name of Jesus.
7. What was Paul's view of his death?
8. What do we learn about God from these verses?

Memory Verse: II Timothy 4:7-8

Grapevine Studies
Old Testament

C/E Cards
Level 3

PAUL

Character/Event Cards

Create a card for Paul.

> - *Saul and Paul are the same man.*
> - *Paul's mission in life was to preach the gospel to the Gentiles, Jews and to kings.*
> - *Paul wrote many of the New Testament epistles.*

Paul

Write your memory verse:

II Timothy 4:7-8

Level 2

Memory Work: Continue to memorize the Apostle's Creed.

2005

SP 154

LETTERS TO THE CHURCHES

Timeline Review

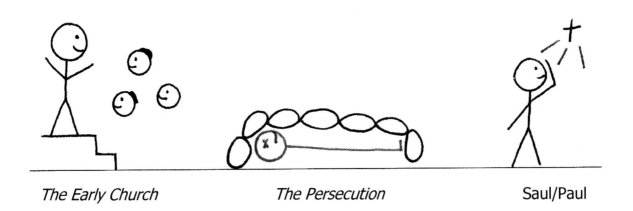

The Early Church   *The Persecution*   *Saul/Paul*

Bible Verses

II Timothy 4:7-8

Acts 9:15-16

Grapevine Studies
New Testament

Lesson 33
Level 1-2

LETTERS TO THE CHURCHES (Part 1)

Background Bible Reading: Various
Time Frame: The early Church

The Letters to the Churches: *We will cover the books of the New Testament in the order that they appear in our Bibles. In the top left corner of the "envelope" I have listed the author and the biblical "address." In the center of the envelope I have listed to whom the letter was written to and the biblical address. I recommend locating the Churches on a map. This is a great opportunity to explain to your students how the canon of scripture was developed and why some books were chosen and others rejected.*

See notes on page opposing page.

LETTERS TO THE CHURCHES

Bible Verses: Various
Time Frame: The Early Church

The purpose of the letters to the Churches was to *teach, exhort, correct,* and *encourage* believers.

Paul
Romans 1:1

Church at Rome
Romans 1:7

Romans

Paul
I Corinthians 1:1

Church at Corinth
I Corinthians 1:2

I Corinthians

Paul
II Corinthians 1:1

Church at Corinth
II Corinthians 1:1

II Corinthians

Paul
Galatians 1:1

Church in Galatia
Galatians 1:2

Galatians

Paul
Ephesians 1:1

Church at Ephesus
Ephesians 1:1

Ephesians

Paul
Philippians 1:1

Church at Philippi
Philippians 1:1

Philippians

Grapevine Studies
New Testament

Lesson 33
Level 1-2

LETTERS TO THE CHURCHES (Part 1)

Letters to the Churches: *See notes on page opposing page.*

1. Why were the letters written to the Churches? *To teach, exhort, correct and encourage believers.*
2. Name four books written by Paul. *See lesson.*
3. Who were the three authors of the books to the Church at Thessalonica? *Paul, Silvanus, and Timothy.*

2005

Grapevine Studies Lesson 33
New Testament Level 1-2

```
┌─────────────────────────┐
│ Paul                 ☐  │
│ Colossians 1:1          │
│                         │
│    Church at Colosse    │
│    Colossians 1:2       │
│                         │
└─────────────────────────┘
        Colossians
```

```
┌─────────────────────────────┐
│ Paul, Silvanus, & Timothy ☐ │
│ I Thessalonians 1:1         │
│                             │
│    Church at Thessalonica   │
│    I Thessalonians 1:1      │
│                             │
└─────────────────────────────┘
        I Thessalonians
```

```
┌─────────────────────────────┐
│ Paul, Silvanus, & Timothy ☐ │
│ II Thessalonians 1:1        │
│                             │
│    Church at Thessalonica   │
│    II Thessalonians 1:1     │
│                             │
└─────────────────────────────┘
        II Thessalonians
```

```
┌─────────────────────────┐
│ Paul                 ☐  │
│ I Timothy 1:1           │
│                         │
│         Timothy         │
│         I Timothy 1:2   │
│                         │
└─────────────────────────┘
        I Timothy
```

```
┌─────────────────────────┐
│ Paul                 ☐  │
│ II Timothy 1:1          │
│                         │
│         Timothy         │
│         II Timothy 1:2  │
│                         │
└─────────────────────────┘
        II Timothy
```

Lesson Review

1. Why were the letters written to the Churches?
2. Name four books written by Paul.
3. Who were the three authors of the books to the Church at Thessalonica?

Memory Verse: II Timothy 3:16-17

SP 157

Grapevine Studies
Old Testament

C/E Cards
Level 3

LETTERS TO THE CHURCHES

Character/Event Cards

Create a card for the Letters to the Churches.

- *The New Testament epistles/letters were written to Churches and individuals.*
- *The epistles were meant to correct, encourage, exhort and teach.*
- *There are twenty-two New Testament epistles.*
- *Paul wrote thirteen of the New Testament epistles.*

The Letters to the Churches

Write your memory verse:

II Timothy 3:16-17

Memory Work: Continue to memorize the Apostle's Creed.

2005

SP 158

Grapevine Studies
New Testament
Review
Level 1-2

LETTERS TO THE CHURCHES

Timeline Review

The Persecution *Saul/Paul* Letters to the Churches

Bible Verses

II Timothy 3:16-17

II Timothy 4:7-8

2005

SP 159

Grapevine Studies
New Testament

Lesson 34
Level 1-2

LETTERS TO THE CHURCHES (Part 2)

Background Bible Reading: Various
Time Frame: The early Church

The Letters to the Churches: *We will cover the books of the New Testament in the order that they appear in our Bibles. In the top left corner of the "envelope" I have listed the author and the biblical "address". In the center of the envelope I have listed who the letter was written to and the biblical address. I recommend locating the Churches on a map.*

See notes on page opposing page.

Grapevine Studies
New Testament

Lesson 34
Level 1-2

LETTERS TO THE CHURCHES

Bible Verses: Various
Time Frame: The early Church

The purpose of the letters to the Churches was to *teach, exhort, correct* and *encourage* believers.

Paul Titus 1:1 *Titus* Titus 1:4	*Paul* Philemon 1:1 *Philemon* Philemon 1:1
Titus	**Philemon**
Unknown *General letter to the Church*	*James* James 1:1 *Twelve tribes who are scattered* James 1:1
Hebrews	**James**
Peter I Peter 1:1 *Pilgrims of the dispersion* I Peter 1:1	*Peter* II Peter 1:1 *General letter to the Church* II Peter 1:1
I Peter	**II Peter**

2005

SP 160

Grapevine Studies
New Testament

Lesson 34
Level 1-2

LETTERS TO THE CHURCHES (Part 2)

Letters to the Churches: *The book of Revelation was written by John while he was exiled on the island of Patmos (Revelation 1:9).*

See notes on page opposing page.

1. Which New Testament letters were written to Churches? See lesson.
2. Which New Testament letters were written to individuals? See lesson.

Grapevine Studies
New Testament
Lesson 34
Level 1-2

John

General letter to the Church

I John

The Elder
II John 1:1

The elect lady and her children
II John 1:1

II John

The Elder
III John 1:1

Gaius
III John 1:1

III John

Jude
Jude 1:1

General letter to the Church
Jude 1:1

Jude

Jesus through John
Revelation 1:1

Churches of Revelation
Revelation 1:4
- Ephesus 2:1
- Smyrna 2:8
- Pergamos 2:12
- Thyatira 2:18
- Sardis 3:1
- Philadelphia 3:7
- Laodicea 3:14

Revelation

Lesson Review

Which New Testament letters were written to Churches?

Which New Testament letters were written to individuals?

Memory Verse: Romans 15:4

SP 161

Grapevine Studies
Old Testament

C/E Cards
Level 3

LETTERS TO THE CHURCHES

Character/Event Cards

Continue to add to the card for the Letters to the Churches.

> - *Record information about the letters to the Churches that you deem important for your students to remember.*

The Letters to the Churches

Write your memory verse:

Romans 15:4

Level 2

Memory Work: Continue to memorize the Apostle's Creed.

2005

SP 162

THE GOSPEL IN STICK FIGURES

Timeline Review

The Persecution   *Saul/Paul*   Letters to the Churches

Bible Verses

Romans 15:4

II Timothy 3:16-17

Grapevine Studies
New Testament

Lesson 35
Level 1-2

THE GOSPEL IN STICK FIGURES

Background Bible Reading: Various
Time Frame: Current

Teachers: *During this lesson, we would like to review the Gospel from Creation to Judgment. I have given only one verse at each point, with my desire being that teachers and students would add their own verses to this outline.*

Creation: *At Creation the relationship between God and man was complete and unbroken.*

Draw the God triangle with a complete line to man's heart.

Sin: *When Adam and Eve ate the forbidden fruit, sin entered all of Creation, and the relationship between God and man was broken. All men born since this time have been born with a broken relationship to God.*

Draw a triangle with a broken line and sin written in the broken place.

The Promise: *Although God punished Adam and Eve for their sin, He did not leave them without a hope and a promise. In Genesis 3:15 God told Adam that one day Messiah would come and restore the broken relationship between God and man. Throughout the New Testament we looked forward to a Messiah who would be born of woman, born of the line of Abraham, and born of the line of David.*

Draw two eyes looking forward.

Messiah: *In the fullness of time Messiah was born, and His name was Jesus.*

Draw the manger.

Sinless Life: *When Jesus lived on earth He was tempted, just as we are, yet lived His life without sin.*

Draw sin with a circle around it.

2005 by Grapevine Studies

Grapevine Studies
New Testament

Lesson 35
Level 1-2

I Corinthian 15:1-5

THE GOSPEL

Creation	Sin	The Promise	The Messiah	Sinless Life
Genesis 1:31	Genesis 3:6	Genesis 3:15	Galatians 4:4-5	Hebrews 4:15

SP 164

Grapevine Studies
New Testament

Lesson 35
Level 1-2

THE GOSPEL IN STICK FIGURES

Died and Buried: *Scripture records that Jesus was scourged, beaten, and then crucified. After Jesus died, He was buried.*

Draw the tomb with Jesus in it.

Rose and Ascended: *Three days after Jesus died and was buried, He rose from the grave. After appearing to many people, He ascended to Heaven, where He sits at the right hand of God interceding for us.*

Draw the resurrection.

Restored: *Through Jesus' death, burial, and resurrection, the relationship between God and man can be restored.*

⬆ propiation   *Draw the God triangle and heart of man connected by a cross.*

Coming Again: *Scripture tells us that Jesus will come again.*

Draw the Jesus cross with an arrow pointing down.

Judgment: *All men will one day stand before Jesus to be judged.*

Draw a purple cross with a man bowing down.

2005

Grapevine Studies
New Testament

Lesson 35
Level 1-2

THE GOSPEL

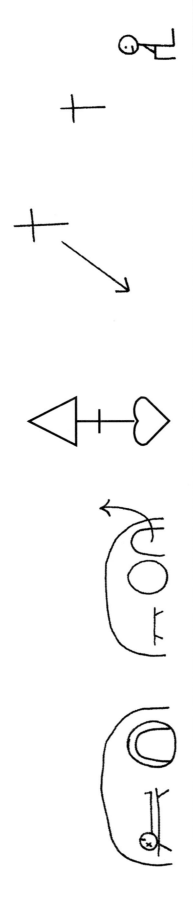
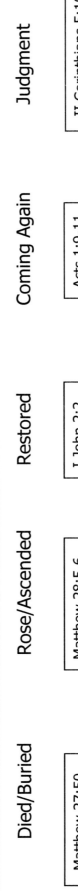
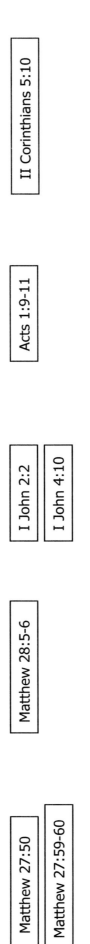

Died/Buried	Rose/Ascended	Restored	Coming Again	Judgment
Matthew 27:50	Matthew 28:5-6	I John 2:2	Acts 1:9-11	II Corinthians 5:10
Matthew 27:59-60		I John 4:10		

Memory Verse: Matthew 24:14

2005

255

SP 165

Grapevine Studies
Old Testament

C/E Cards
Level 3

THE GOSPEL IN STICK FIGURES

Character/Event Cards

Create a card for the Gospel.

- *The main points of the Gospel:*
    1. *Creation*
    2. *Sin*
    3. *The Promise*
    4. *The Messiah*
    5. *Sinless Life*
    6. *Died*
    7. *Buried*
    8. *Rose*
    9. *Ascended*
    10. *Restored*
    11. *Coming Again*
    12. *Judgment*

The Gospel

Write your memory verse:

Matthew 24:14

Level 2

Memory Work: Continue to memorize the Apostle's Creed.

Grapevine Studies
New Testament

Review
Level 1-2

SHARING THE GOSPEL

Timeline Review

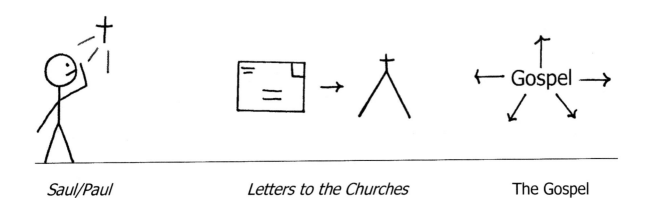

Saul/Paul   Letters to the Churches   The Gospel

Bible Verses

Matthew 24:14

Romans 15:4

2005

SP 167

Grapevine Studies
New Testament

Lesson 36
Level 1-2

SHARING THE GOSPEL

Background Bible Reading: Various
Time Frame: Current

Teachers: *During this lesson I would like to continue the Gospel, showing how to make it personal. I have given only a verse or two at each point, with my desire being that teachers and students would add their own verses to this outline.*

I Am a Sinner: *It is important for each of us to understand that we are all sinners.*

Draw yourself.

Jesus Died for Me: *Jesus died for my sins.*

Draw Jesus on the cross.

I Need to Repent: *Repent means to agree with God about my sin.*

Draw yourself walking away from God and then an arrow pointing toward God.

I Can Receive God's Forgiveness: *As a sinner, when I sincerely repent, God has promised that I will be forgiven.*

Draw a man praying and the God triangle and man's heart connected with a cross.

Grapevine Studies
New Testament

Lesson 36
Level 1-2

I Corinthian 15:1-7

SHARING THE GOSPEL

I am a Sinner	Jesus Died for Me	I Need to Repent	I Can Receive God's Forgiveness
I Corinthians 15:22	John 3:16	Acts 17:30	I John 1:9
Romans 3:23		Acts 3:19	

SP 168

Grapevine Studies
New Testament

Lesson 36
Level 1-2

SHARING THE GOSPEL

Growing in My Faith: *We will look at some of the things the early Church did as an expression of their new faith.*

Learn and Obey Biblical Doctrine: *It is important that we not only learn the Word of God but also be obedient to those things we are taught.*

Draw a Bible.

Continue Fellowship with Other Believers: *Fellowship is a necessary part of growing in the Lord. Through fellowship we learn, we are challenged and we are corrected.*

Draw two people talking together.

Pray both in Private and with Other Believers: *Communicating with our God is essential to growth.*

Draw two men praying.

Celebrate Communion: *We need to regularly be reminded of the great price that was paid for our salvation.*

Draw a man with bread and wine.

Be Baptized: *Baptism is an important public acknowledgement of our faith.*

Draw a man being baptized.

Share the Gospel: *Find effective ways to communicate the love of God to our family, friends and others.*

Draw two men talking.

1. Why is obedience to biblical doctrine important? *Obedience shows our love for God.*
2. How does fellowship help us to grow in faith? *Through encouragement, correction, and exhortation.*
3. What are two ways we can pray? *In private and with others.*
4. What do we remember when we celebrate communion? *The Lord's death and the New Covenant in His blood.*
5. Why should I be baptized? *In obedience to the Lord.*
6. What do we learn about God from these verses? *God wants us to grow in our faith.*

©2005

Grapevine Studies
New Testament

Lesson 36
Level 1-2

Acts 2:42

Acts 2:38

Growing in My Faith

1. Learn and Obey Biblical Doctrine

2. Fellowship with other Believers

3. Pray both in Private and with Other Believers

4. Celebrate Communion

5. Be Baptized

6. Share the Gospel

Lesson Review

1. Why is obedience to biblical doctrine important?
2. How does fellowship help us to grow in faith?
3. What are two ways we can pray?
4. What do we remember when we celebrate communion?
5. Why should I be baptized?
6. What do we learn about God from these verses?

Memory Verse: James 1:22

SP 169

Review 6

1. What happened to the Church after Stephen was stoned? *The Church entered a time of persecution, which caused the believers to scatter and preach the Gospel in new areas.*

2. What role did Saul play in the persecution of the Church? *Saul was one of the main persecutors of the early Church.*

3. What happened to Saul on the road to Damascus? *The Lord appeared to Saul, and he was struck blind and believed that Jesus was the Messiah.*

4. Who was Ananias? *A believer from Damascus to whom the Lord spoke and who prayed for Saul to receive his sight.*

5. How did Saul leave Damascus? *In a basket, let down over the city wall.*

6. When Saul returned to Jerusalem, how was he received by the disciples, Barnabas, and the apostles? *The disciples doubted his conversion, while Barnabas and the apostles believed that Saul had truly become a believer.*

7. Why did Barnabas and Saul go to Antioch, and what did they do there? *They went to verify the fact that many Jews had become believers there, and they stayed to teach the people.*

8. Recite Acts 9:15-16

9. What was Paul's mission from God? *To preach the Gospel to the Gentiles, to kings, and to the Jews.*

10. What other name was Paul known by? *Saul.*

11. What was the response of the Gentiles when Paul preached? *Many received the Word with gladness and glorified the Lord.*

12. What was the response of King Agrippa to Paul's preaching? *He was almost persuaded.*

13. What was the response of the Jews to Paul's preaching? *Some opposed but some believed, including the ruler of the synagogue.*

14. Name some of the things Paul suffered for the name of Jesus. *Stoning, shipwreck, and beatings.*

Grapevine Studies
New Testament
Review 6
Level 1-2

15. What was Paul's view of his death? *He looked forward to the crown of righteousness.*
16. Recite II Timothy 4:7-8.
17. Why were the letters written to the Churches? *To teach, exhort, correct and encourage believers.*
18. Who were the three authors of the books to the Church at Thessalonica? *Paul, Silvanus, and Timothy.*
19. Recite II Timothy 3:16-17.
20. Which New Testament letters were written to Churches? *See lessons.*
21. Which New Testament letters were written to individuals? *See lessons.*
22. Recite Romans 15:4.
23. Give the main points of the Gospel outline. *Creation, Sin, The Promise, The Messiah, Sinless Life, Died, Buried, Rose, Ascended, Restored, Coming Again, Judgment.*
24. Recite Matthew 24:14.
25. Why is obedience to biblical doctrine important? *Obedience shows our love for God.*
26. How does fellowship help us to grow in faith? *Through encouragement, correction, and exhortation.*
27. What are two ways we can pray? *In private and with others.*
28. What do we remember when we celebrate communion? *The Lord's death and the New Covenant in His blood.*
29. Why should I be baptized? *In obedience to the Lord.*
30. Recite James 1:22.

Level 2

31. Name the books of the New Testament. *Matthew, Mark, Luke John, Acts, Romans, I & II Corinthians, Galatians, Ephesians, Philippians, Colossians, I & II Thessalonians, I & II Timothy, Titus, Philemon, Hebrews, James, I & II Peter, I, II & III John, Jude, and Revelation.*
32. Name The Twelve Apostles. *Andrew, Simon (Peter), Phillip, Matthew (Levi), James, John, Bartholomew, Thomas, James (son of Alphaeus), Lebbaeus, Simon (the Canaanite), and Judas Iscariot.*
33. Recite the as much of The Apostles Creed as possible. *See page 307.*

2005
SP 171

Section 8 Goals and Key Points

THE SEALS, TRUMPETS AND BOWLS

The goal of this lesson is briefly introduce students to some of the events that will take place during the time known as the Great Tribulation.

Key Points:
- Mankind and Creation will experience great tribulation when the:
    1. The seven seals are opened.
    2. The seven bowls are poured out.
    3. The seven trumpets are sounded.
- During the Great Tribulation, men will refuse to repent.

THE SECOND COMING OF JESUS

The goal of this lesson is to show what events will surround the second coming of Jesus Christ.

Key Points:
- Kings will gather their men to Armageddon to fight against God.
- Jesus will return and defeat the armies gathered against Him.
- Satan will be bound in the bottomless pit for the Millennium.
- During the Millennium, Jesus will reign over the earth.
- At the end of the Millennium, Satan will be released and will deceive mankind again.
- Jesus will defeat all His enemies at the final battle.

HELL

The goal of this lesson is to look at the facts regarding the place called Hell.

Key Points:
- All men will be judged.
- At the Great White Throne Judgment, the books will be opened.
- Anyone whose name is not found in the Book of Life will be thrown into the lake of fire and brimstone.
- Jesus will separate the believers from the unbelievers at the end of time.
- Hell was originally a place prepared for Satan and his demons.

Grapevine Studies
New Testament

Section 8
Level 1-2

HEAVEN

The goal of this lesson is to show what a glorious place heaven will be.

Key Points:
- Men will think that Jesus is not coming because God is patient, not wanting men to die without repenting.
- God will destroy the old earth and heaven with fire and bring forth a new heaven and new earth.
- Heaven will be a place of:
  1. No tears
  2. No death
  3. No sorrow
  4. No crying
  5. No pain
  6. God dwelling among His people.
- The book of Revelation has a blessing at the beginning and a warning at the end.
  1. Anyone who reads or hears the book of Revelation will be blessed.
  2. Anyone who adds to or deletes from the book of Revelation will be cursed.

Grapevine Studies
Old Testament

C/E Cards
Level 3

SHARING THE GOSPEL

Character/Event Cards

Create a card for Sharing the Gospel.

> - The main points of understanding the Gospel are:
>   1. I am a sinner.
>   2. Jesus died for me.
>   3. I need to repent.
>   4. I can receive God's forgiveness.
>
> - I can grow in my faith by:
>   1. Leaning and obeying the Bible.
>   2. Fellowshipping with other believers.
>   3. Praying.
>   4. Celebrating Communion.
>   5. Being Baptized.
>   6. Sharing the Gospel.

Sharing the Gospel

Write your memory verse:

James 1:22

Level 2

Memory Work: Continue to memorize the Apostle's Creed.

2005

SP 172

THE SEALS, TRUMPETS, AND BOWLS

Timeline Review

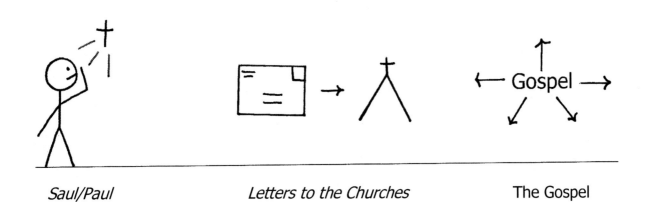

Saul/Paul   Letters to the Churches   The Gospel

Bible Verses

James 1:22

Matthew 24:14

Grapevine Studies
New Testament

Lesson 37
Level 1-2

THE SEALS, TRUMPETS, AND BOWLS (Part 1)

Background Bible Reading: Revelation 1-11
Time Frame: The Great Tribulation

The Lamb and the Scroll: *John sees a scene in heaven in which there is a scroll at the right hand of God, but no one is worthy to open the scroll except Jesus.*

scroll, seals   *Draw a scroll with seven seals.*

Seal 1: *The first seal is a white horse with a rider who is given a crown and has a bow.*

Draw a crown and a bow.

Seal 2: *The second seal is a fiery red horse whose rider is given a great sword and is sent to take peace from the earth.*

Draw a sword and write "No Peace."

Seal 3: *The third seal is a black horse whose rider is holding a pair of scales.*

Draw a pair of scales.

Seal 4: *The fourth seal is represented by a pale horse whose rider is death, followed by Hades, and power is given to kill one fourth of the earth by sword, hunger, pestilence, and wild beasts.*

Draw the earth and mark ¼ dead.

Seal 5: *When the fifth seal is opened, the souls of those who had been killed because of their faith in Jesus are seen crying out and asking the Lord how long until God judges and avenges.*

Draw a man crying out to God.

Grapevine Studies
New Testament

Lesson 37
Level 1-2

THE SEALS, TRUMPETS, AND BOWLS

Bible Verses: Revelation 5:1-7; 6:1-17; 8:1-13
Time Frame: The Great Tribulation

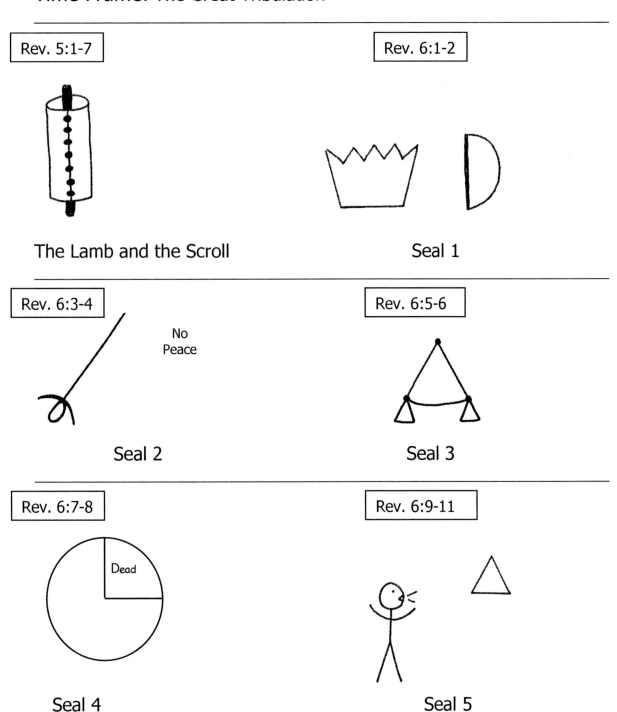

SP 174

Grapevine Studies
New Testament
Lesson 37
Level 1-2

THE SEALS, TRUMPETS, AND BOWLS (Part 1)

Seal 6: *At the breaking of the sixth seal there is a great earthquake, the sun becomes like sackcloth, the moon, like blood, and the stars fall from heaven. The sky is split apart, every mountain and island is moved, and all men hide themselves in caves from the One who sits on the Throne.*

Draw a darkened sun, blood, red moon, and falling stars.

Seal 7: *When the seventh seal is broken there is silence in heaven and seven angels are given seven trumpets. Another angel throws a censor to earth and as a result there is noise, lightnings, thunders and an earthquake.*

Draw noise, thunders, and lightning, and label "silence."

Trumpet 1: *The first trumpet sounds, and fire and hail fall to the earth and burn up 1/3 of the trees and all the grass of the earth.*

 trumpets   *Draw 1/3 of a tree burning and 1/3 of the grass burning.*

Trumpet 2: *The second trumpeted sounds, and a mountain-like object is thrown into the sea causing 1/3 of the sea to become blood, killing 1/3 of the sea creatures and destroying 1/3 of the ships.*

Write 1/3 of the sea bloody, 1/3 of the sea creatures dead, and 1/3 of the ships sunk.

Trumpet 3: *The third trumpet sounds, and a great star falls from heaven and makes 1/3 of the rivers and springs bitter, causing men to die.*

Draw a river and spring and a dead man.

Trumpet 4: *The fourth trumpet sounded and 1/3 of the sun, moon, and stars are darkened.*

Draw the sun, moon, and three stars darkened.

1. Who is worthy to open the seals? *The Lamb Jesus.*
2. What are the seven seals? *See lesson.*
3. What are the first four trumpets? *See lesson.*
4. What do we learn about God from these verses? *There will come a time when judgment will come on the earth.*

Grapevine Studies
New Testament

Lesson 37
Level 1-2

Rev. 6:12-17

Rev. 8:1-5

Silence

Seal 6

Seal 7

Rev. 8:6-7

Rev. 8:8-9

1/3 Sea becomes blood

1/3 Sea creatures die

1/3 Ships sink

Trumpet 1

Trumpet 2

Rev. 8:10-11

Rev. 8:12-13

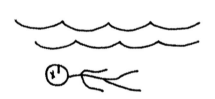

Trumpet 3

Trumpet 4

Lesson Review

1. Who is worthy to open the seals?
2. What are the seven seals?
3. What are the first four trumpet judgments?
4. What do we learn about God from these verses?

Memory Verse: Revelation 5:9

2005

SP 175

Grapevine Studies
Old Testament

C/E Cards
Level 3

THE SEALS, TRUMPETS, AND BOWLS

Character/Event Cards

Create a card for the Seals, Trumpets, and Bowls.

> - *The mankind and creation will experience great tribulation when the:*
>   1. *The seven Seals are opened.*
>   2. *The seven Bowls are poured out.*
>   3. *The seven Trumpets are sounded.*
>
> - *During The Great Tribulation men will refuse to repent.*

The Seals, Trumpets, and Bowls

Write your memory verse:

Revelation 5:9

Level 2

Memory Work: Continue to memorize the Apostle's Creed.

SP 176

Grapevine Studies
New Testament

Review
Level 1-2

THE SEALS, TRUMPETS, AND BOWLS

Timeline Review

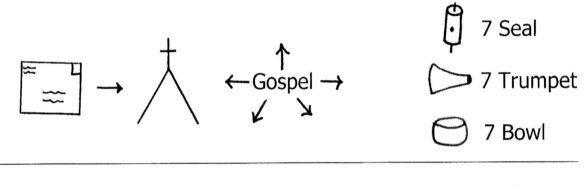

Letters to the Churches   *The Gospel*   *The Great Tribulation*

Bible Verses

Revelation 5:9

James 1:22

2005

SP 177

Grapevine Studies
New Testament

Lesson 38
Level 1-2

THE SEALS, TRUMPETS, AND BOWLS (Part 2)

Background Bible Reading: Revelation 12-16
Time Frame: The Great Tribulation

Trumpet 5: *The fifth trumpet sounds and the bottomless pit is opened. Out of the pit come smoke and locusts. These locusts are given instructions not to harm those who have the seal of God on their foreheads but to torment men for five months. The tormented men will seek escape through death but will be unable to escape.*

👆 locusts   *Draw a pit with locust, coming out and a man running.*

Trumpet 6: *The sixth trumpet releases four angels, who kill 1/3 of mankind.*

Draw four angels and note 1/3 of mankind is killed.

Mankind Refuses to Repent: *Although many plagues have been sent upon the earth in judgment, mankind still refuses to repent of their wicked deeds.*

👆 repent   *Draw a circle and "repent."*

Trumpet 7: *The last trumpet begins with an announcement and heavenly worship of God. Then the temple of God in heaven is opened and the ark of His covenant is seen in the heavenly temple. This event is accompanied by lightning, thunder, earthquake, noise, and large hail.*

Draw the ark in a cloud and lightning, thunder, and hail.

The Mark of the Beast: *As the beast of Revelation comes to power, he performs many convincing signs and miracles. He also makes all of mankind receive a mark in order to buy or sell.*

👆 signs, worship, mark   *Draw a man with a mark on his forehead and a mark on his hand*

Bowl 1: *The first bowl is poured out, causing sores on all those who have the mark of the beast or worship him.*

👆 wrath   *Draw a man with sores.*

2005

Grapevine Studies
New Testament

Lesson 38
Level 1-2

THE SEALS, TRUMPETS, AND BOWLS

Bible Verses: Various Revelation Passages
Time Frame: The Great Tribulation

Rev. 9:1-5	Rev. 9:13-19
	1/3 Mankind
Trumpet 5	Trumpet 6

Rev. 9:20-21	Rev. 11:15-16, 19

Mankind Refuses to Repent	Trumpet 7

Rev. 13:11-18	Rev. 15:7-8, 16:1-2

The Mark of the Beast	Bowl 1

Grapevine Studies
New Testament

Lesson 38
Level 1-2

THE SEALS, TRUMPETS, AND BOWLS (Part 2)

Bowl 2: *The second bowl is poured out, the sea turns to blood, and all the sea creatures die.*

Draw a blood, sea and dead sea creatures.

Bowl 3: *The third bowl is poured out, and the rivers and springs turn to blood.*

Draw a bloody river and a bloody springs.

Bowl 4: *When the fourth bowl is poured out, men are scorched with heat but blaspheme God and still refuse to repent.*

Draw the sun beating down on a man.

Bowl 5: *The fifth bowl strikes the throne of the beast and causes darkness and pain to men, but men respond by blaspheming God.*

Draw darkness and a man in pain.

Bowl 6: *The sixth bowl is poured out causing the Euphrates River to dry up. Out of the river come demon creatures, who gather men from all over the world to battle in a place called Armageddon.*

Draw a man with a shield.

Bowl 7: *The last bowl begins with the proclamation "It is done." Thunders, lightning, and earthquakes more powerful than any before strike. Mountains and islands flee away and giant hailstones fall.*

Draw thunder, lightning, and a man running from large hail.

1. What are the last three trumpets? *See lesson.*
2. How does mankind respond to the seals, bowls, and trumpets? *They blaspheme God and refuse to repent of their sins.*
3. What are the seven bowls? *See lesson.*
4. Why would men want to take the mark of the beast? *To be able to buy and sell.*
5. What do we learn about God from these verses? *There will come a time when God's stored-up wrath will be released.*

Grapevine Studies
New Testament

Lesson 38
Level 1-2

Rev. 16:3

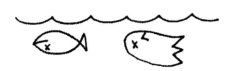

Bowl 2

Rev. 16:4-7

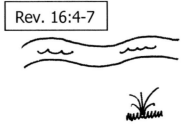

Bowl 3

Rev. 16:8-9

Bowl 4

Rev. 16:10-11

Bowl 5

Rev. 16:12-16

Bowl 6

Rev. 16:17-21

Bowl 7

Lesson Review

1. What are the last three trumpets?
2. How does mankind respond to the seals, bowls, and trumpets?
3. What are the seven bowls?
4. Why would men want to take the mark of the beast?
5. What do we learn about God from these verses?

Memory Verse: Revelation 9:20

2005

SP 179

Grapevine Studies
Old Testament

C/E Cards
Level 3

THE SEALS, TRUMPETS, AND BOWLS

Character/Event Cards

Continue to add to the card for the Seals, Trumpets, and Bowls.

> - *Record information about the Great Tribulation that you deem important for your students to remember.*

The Seals, Trumpets, and Bowls

Write your memory verse:

Revelation 9:20

Level 2

Memory Work: Continue to memorize the Apostle's Creed.

2005

SP 180

Grapevine Studies · New Testament — Review Level 1-2

THE SECOND COMING OF JESUS

Timeline Review

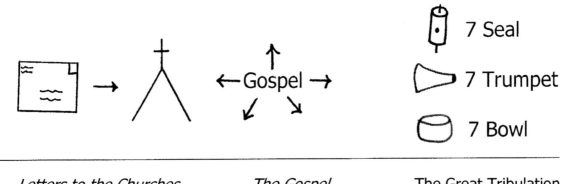

Letters to the Churches 　　 The Gospel 　　 The Great Tribulation

Bible Verses

Revelation 9:20

Revelation 5:9

Grapevine Studies
New Testament

Lesson 39
Level 1-2

THE SECOND COMING OF JESUS

Background Bible Reading: Revelation 16-20
Time Frame: The end of the Great Tribulation

Armageddon: *During the last two lessons we have studied the events often called the "Great Tribulation." One of the events we looked at, the sixth bowl, sets the stage for the coming of Jesus. Demonic forces are unleashed and gather the kings of the earth and their armies to a place called Armageddon.*

⌂ signs, Armageddon   *Draw army men following a king.*

Jesus Returns: *This passage is a stunning description of Jesus as He comes to exercise judgment against the nations. (Revelation 1:7)*

⌂ judges, war   *Draw Jesus with dead enemies.*

The World Armies Are Defeated: *When Jesus returns, those who are gathered to fight against Him are completely destroyed.*

Draw dead army men.

Satan Is Chained: *The return of Jesus culminates with Satan being chained by an angel and thrown into the bottomless pit, where he will remain for 1,000 years.*

⌂ bottomless pit   *Draw Satan chained to the bottomless pit.*

2005

Grapevine Studies
New Testament

Lesson 39
Level 1-2

THE SECOND COMING OF JESUS

Bible Verses: Revelation 16:12-16; 19:11-21; 20:1-10
Time Frame: The end of the Great Tribulation

Rev. 16:12-16

Rev. 19:11-16

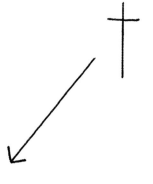

Armageddon

Jesus Returns

Rev. 19:17-21

Rev. 20:1-3

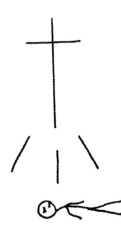

The World Armies Are Defeated

Satan Is Chained

2005

SP 182

Grapevine Studies
New Testament

Lesson 39
Level 1-2

THE SECOND COMING OF JESUS

The Millennium: *During the Millennium (or 1,000 years), after the return of Jesus Christ, the saints reign with Him over the earth.*

☝ millennium, reign, resurrection   *Draw Jesus on a throne.*

Satan Is Released: *When the Millennium is completed, Satan will be released from the bottomless pit to deceive mankind once more.*

Draw Satan, with a broken chain, talking to a man.

Satan's Final Battle: *Once Satan is released, he will deceives the nations and gather men for battle. When Satan's army surrounds the "camp of the saints" and the "beloved city," God will respond by sending fire from heaven to destroy them all.*

☝ saints   *Draw dead men around a city.*

Satan's End: *Satan's end is in the lake of fire, where he will remain for eternity.*

☝ tormented   *Draw Satan in the lake of fire.*

1. What is Armageddon? *A battlefield located in northern Israel in which the kings of the earth will gather their armies and be defeated at the coming of Jesus Christ.*
2. Describe the second coming of Jesus. *Answers will vary.*
3. During the Millennium over, who is reining, the earth? *Jesus and the saints.*
4. During the Millennium, where is Satan? *Chained to the bottomless pit.*
5. What happens at the end of the Millennium? *Satan is released and deceives man again.*
6. What is Satan's end? *The lake of fire for eternity.*
7. What do we learn about God from these verses? *Jesus will demonstrate with His return and throughout the Millennium that His power and justice are absolute.*

2005

Grapevine Studies
New Testament

Lesson 39
Level 1-2

Rev. 20:4-6

The Millennium

Rev. 20:7-8

Satan Is Released

Rev. 20:9

Satan's Final battle

Rev. 20:10

Satan's End

Lesson Review

1. What is Armageddon?
2. Describe the second coming of Jesus.
3. During the Millennium over, who is reining the earth?
4. During the Millennium, where is Satan?
5. What happens at the end of the Millennium?
6. What is Satan's end?
7. What do we learn about God from these verses?

Memory Verse: Revelation 1:7 Behold,

2005

SP 183

Grapevine Studies
Old Testament

C/E Cards
Level 3

THE SECOND COMING OF JESUS

Character/Event Cards

Create a card for the Second Coming.

> - *Kings will gather their men to Armageddon to fight against God.*
> - *Jesus will return and defeat the armies gather against Him.*
> - *Satan will be bound in the bottomless pit for the Millennium.*
> - *During the Millennium, Jesus will reign over the earth.*
> - *At the end of the Millennium, Satan will be released and will deceive mankind again.*

The Second Coming

Write your memory verse:

Revelation 1:7

Level 2

Memory Work: Continue to memorize the Apostle's Creed.

2005

SP 184

Grapevine Studies
New Testament

Review
Level 1-2

HELL

Timeline Review

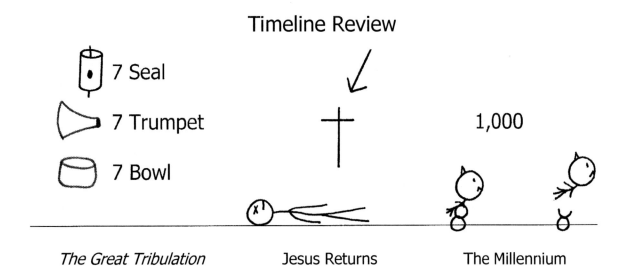

Bible Verses

Revelation 1:7

Revelation 9:20

2005

SP 185

Grapevine Studies
New Testament

Lesson 40
Level 1-2

HELL

Background Bible Reading: Revelation 20-21
Time Frame: Eternity

All Mankind Will Be Judged: *These two passages make it clear that each person will be judged, whether believer or unbeliever.*

 Judgment, account   *Draw a man kneeling before Jesus.*

The Great White Throne Judgment: *At the Great White Throne Judgment, the books will be opened and those not recorded in the Book of Life will be thrown into the lake of fire.*

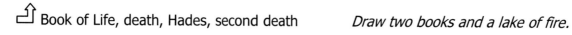 Book of Life, death, Hades, second death   *Draw two books and a lake of fire.*

Separating the Sheep and the Goats: *While Jesus was on the earth, He describe what Judgment would be like. The sheep represent believers, and the goats represent unbelievers. The believers will go to eternal life in the presence of God, but the unbelievers will be condemned to eternal punishment.*

Draw Jesus with one happy man on His right and one sad man on His left.

2005

HELL

Bible Verses: Various
Time Frame: Eternity

Rom. 14:10-12
II Cor. 5:10

Rev. 20:11-15
Rev. 21:8

  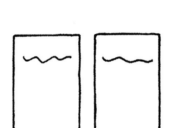 

All Mankind Will Be Judged   The Great White Throne Judgment

Rev. 19:17-21
Matt. 31-34, 41, 46

Rev. 21:1-3

Separating the Sheep and the Goats

SP 186

Grapevine Studies
New Testament
Lesson 40
Level 1-2

HELL

The Rich Man and Lazarus: *After the death of every man comes judgment. The story of the rich man and Lazarus is an example of the finality of this judgment.*

 Abraham's bosom   *Draw the rich man in hell and Lazarus in heaven.*

Hell's Original Purpose: *Hell was designed as a place of punishment for the devil and his angels. Even the demons are aware that their judgment awaits them.*

Draw Satan in the lake of fire.

A Description of Hell: *A place of torment, outer darkness, weeping, gnashing of teeth, fire that is never quenched, lake of fire and brimstone.*

 torment   *Draw one of the of descriptions of hell.*

1. Who will be judged at the White Throne? *All mankind.*
2. Who will be condemned to hell? *Anyone whose name is not found in the Book of Life.*
3. What did the story about Jesus separating the sheep and the goats represent? *How God will separate believers from unbelievers at the end of time.*
4. What did you learn about Hell from the story of the rich man and Lazarus? *All men will be judged after death; judgment is final; there is no crossing over from hell to heaven or back to earth after judgment.*
5. What was the original purpose for hell? *A place of punishment for Satan and his angels.*
6. Describe hell. *Place of torment, outer darkness, weeping, gnashing of teeth, fire that is never quenched, lake of fire and brimstone.*
7. What do we learn about God from these verses? *God will judge every man, and woe to those who are not found recorded in the Book of Life.*

2005

Grapevine Studies
New Testament

Lesson 40
Level 1-2

Heb. 9:27

Luke 16:19-31

The Rich Man and Lazarus

Rev. 20:8

II Pet. 2:4

Luke 16:23

Matt. 8:12

Mark 9:43

Rev. 20:10, 15

Place of torment
Outer darkness
Weeping
Gnashing of teeth
Fire that is never quenched
Lake of fire and brimstone

Hell's Original Purpose

A Description of Hell

Lesson Review

1. Who will be judged at the White Throne?
2. Who will be condemned to hell?
3. What did the story about Jesus separating the sheep and the goats represent?
4. What did you learn about hell from the story of the rich man and Lazarus?
5. What was the original purpose for hell?
6. Describe hell.
7. What do we learn about God from these verses?

Memory Verse: Revelation 20:15

2005

SP 187

Grapevine Studies
Old Testament

C/E Cards
Level 3

HELL

Character/Event Cards

Create a card for Hell.

> - *All men will be judged.*
> - *At the Great White Throne Judgment, the books will be opened.*
> - *Anyone whose name is not found in the Book of Life will be thrown into the lake of fire and brimstone.*
> - *Jesus will separate the believers from the unbelievers at the end of time.*
> - *Hell was originally a place prepared for Satan and his demons.*

Hell

Write your memory verse:

Revelation 20:15

Level 2

Memory Work: Recite the Apostle's Creed.

2005

SP 188

Grapevine Studies
New Testament

Review
Level 1-2

HEAVEN

Timeline Review

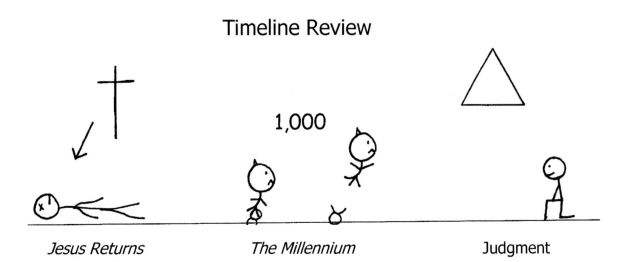

Bible Verses

Revelation 20:15

Revelation 1:7

2005

SP 189

Grapevine Studies
New Testament

Lesson 41
Level 1-2

HEAVEN

Background Bible Reading: Revelation 22
Time Frame: Eternity

God's Patience: *Peter here warns believers that in the last days men will scoff at the thought of Jesus coming again. But Peter reminds us that what appears to us to be a delay is really the patience of God and His desire to see no man perish.*

Draw a man kneeling with an arrow turning around.

New Heaven and New Earth: *Although God is patient; the day will come when the heavens and earth will be replaced with a new heaven and new earth where righteousness will reign.*

⌂ new, holy, godliness   *Draw a new earth.*

God's Dwelling Place: *In this new heaven and new earth, God will once again dwell among His people.*

⌂ tabernacle   *Draw people worshipping God.*

Heaven: *No tears, no death, no sorrow, no crying, no pain, a place where people of every tribe, nation, and tongue will worship God!*

See notes on page opposing page.

2005

Grapevine Studies
New Testament

Lesson 41
Level 1-2

HEAVEN

Bible Verses: Various
Time Frame: Eternity

II Peter 3:1-9

II Peter 3:10-13
Rev. 21:1

God's Patience

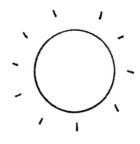

New Heaven and Earth

Rev. 21:2-3

Rev. 21:4   Rev. 5:9
Rev. 7:15-17

No tears
No death
No sorrow
No crying
No pain
A place where people of every tribe, nation, and tongue will worship God!

God's Dwelling Place

A Description of Heaven

SP 190

2005

Grapevine Studies
New Testament

Lesson 41
Level 1-2

HEAVEN

The New Jerusalem: *This is a beautiful description of the New Jerusalem.*

Draw the new Jerusalem.

Final Instructions: *John records these final instructions.*

See notes on page opposing page.

The Blessing and the Warning: *God promises a blessing to those who read and heed the book of Revelation. But God also issues a warning that no words should be added to or take away from this book.*

⌂ blessed, reward, tree of life

Draw a man reading, a page with lines added, and a page with lines deleted.

1. What will men do and say in the last days regarding the return of Jesus? *They will scoff and ask "Where is His coming?"*
2. Why does the second coming appear to be "delayed"? *God is giving time for all men to repent.*
3. What will happen to the current heaven and earth? *They will be destroyed with fire, and there will be a new heaven and new earth.*
4. Describe Heaven: *No tears, no death, no sorrow, no crying, no pain, a place where people of every tribe, nation, and tongue will worship God!*
5. Describe the New Jerusalem. *See lesson.*
6. What are the final instructions of Revelation? *Keep the words of the book, worship God, continue to live a holy and righteous life, and do God's commandments.*
7. What do we learn about God from these verses? *God will one day dwell among His people in heaven.*

2005

Grapevine Studies
New Testament

Lesson 41
Level 1-2

Rev. 21:9-26

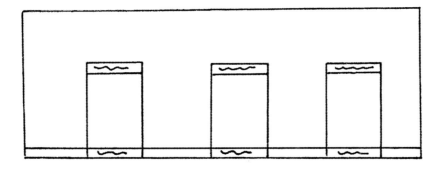

The New Jerusalem

Rev. 22:6-14

Rev. 1:3

Rev. 22:18-20

Keep the words of Revelation

Worship God

Live a righteous life

Do God's commandments

Final Instructions

The Blessing and the Warning

Lesson Review

1. What will men do and say in the last days regarding the return of Jesus?
2. Why does the second coming appear to be "delayed"?
3. What will happen to the current heaven and earth?
4. Describe Heaven.
5. Describe the New Jerusalem.
6. What are the final instructions of Revelation?
7. What do we learn about God from these verses?

Memory Verse: Revelation 21:3

2005

SP 191

Grapevine Studies
New Testament

Quest
Level 3

HEAVEN

Character/Event Cards

Create a card for Heaven.

- Men will think that Jesus is not coming because God is patient, not wanting men to die without repenting.
- God will destroy the old earth and heaven with fire and bring forth a new heaven and new earth.
- Heaven will be a place of:
  1. No tears
  2. No death
  3. No sorrow
  4. No crying
  5. No pain
  6. God dwelling among His people.

Heaven

Write your memory verse:

Revelation 21:3

Level 2

Memory Work: Recite the Apostle's Creed.

2005

SP 192

Grapevine Studies
New Testament

Lesson 42
Level 1-2

Review 7

1. Who is worthy to open the seals? *The Lamb Jesus.*
2. What are the seven seals? *See lesson.*
3. What are the first four trumpets? *See lesson.*
4. Recite Revelation 5:9.
5. What are the last three trumpets? *See lesson.*
6. How does mankind respond to the seals, bowls and trumpets? *They blaspheme God and refuse to repent of their sins.*
7. What are the seven bowls? *See lesson.*
8. Why would men want to take the mark of the beast? *To be able to buy and sell.*
9. Recite Revelation 9:20.
10. What is Armageddon? *A battlefield located in northern Israel in which the kings of the earth will gather their armies and be defeated at the coming of Jesus Christ.*
11. Describe the second coming of Jesus. *Answers will vary.*
12. During the Millennium, who is reining on the earth? *Jesus and the saints.*
13. During the Millennium, where is Satan? *Chained to the bottomless pit.*
14. What happens at the end of the Millennium? *Satan is released and deceives man again.*
15. What is Satan's end? *The lake of fire for eternity.*
16. Recite Revelation 1:7.
17. Who will be judged at the White Throne? *All mankind.*
18. Who will be condemned to hell? *Anyone whose name is not found in the Book of Life.*
19. What did the story about Jesus separating the sheep and the goats represent? *How God will separate believers from unbelievers at the end of time.*
20. What did you learn about Hell from the story of the rich man and Lazarus? *All men will be judged after death; judgment is final; there is no crossing over from hell to heaven or back to earth after judgment.*
21. Describe hell. *Place of torment, outer darkness, weeping, gnashing of teeth, fire that is never quenched, lake of fire and brimstone.*

2005

SP 193

22. What was the original purpose for hell? *A place of punishment for Satan and his angels.*

23. Recite Revelation 20:15.

24. What will men do and say in the last days regarding the return of Jesus? *They will scoff and ask "Where is His coming?"*

25. Why does the second coming appear to be "delayed"? *God is giving time for all men to repent.*

26. What will happen to the current heaven and earth? *They will be destroyed with fire and God and their will be a new heaven and new earth.*

27. Describe the New Jerusalem. *A city built by God for His people.*

28. Describe Heaven. *No tears, no death, no sorrow, no crying, no pain, a place where people of every tribe, nation, and tongue will worship God!*

29. What are the final instructions of Revelation? *Keep the words of the book, worship God, continue to live a holy and righteous life, and do God's commandments.*

30. Recite Revelation 21:3

Level 2

31. Name the books of the New Testament. *Matthew, Mark, Luke John, Acts, Romans, I & II Corinthians, Galatians, Ephesians, Philippians, Colossians, I & II Thessalonians, I & II Timothy, Titus, Philemon, Hebrews, James, I & II Peter, I, II & III John, Jude, and Revelation.*

32. Name The Twelve Apostles. *Andrew, Simon (Peter), Phillip, Matthew (Levi), James, John, Bartholomew, Thomas, James (son of Alphaeus), Lebbaeus, Simon (the Canaanite), and Judas Iscariot.*

33. Recite The Apostles Creed. *See page 307.*

The New Testament Timeline

Final Review

Grapevine Studies
New Testament

Final Review
Level 1-2

New Testament Timeline

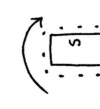

| Birth of John | Birth of Jesus | Jesus in Egypt | Jesus at Age Twelve | Passover |

Grapevine Studies
New Testament

Final Review
Level 1-2

New Testament Timeline

| John Prepared the Way | The Baptism of Jesus | Temptation of Jesus | The Twelve Apostles |

Grapevine Studies
New Testament

Final Review
Level 1-2

New Testament Timeline

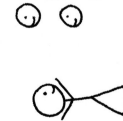

| Jesus Taught | Jesus Prayed | Jesus Calmed the Sea | Jesus Fed the Multitudes |

Grapevine Studies
New Testament

Final Review
Level 1-2

New Testament Timeline

| Jesus Healed the Sick/Lame | Jesus Healed the Demon Possessed | Jesus Raised the Dead |

Grapevine Studies
New Testament

Final Review
Level 1-2

New Testament Timeline

Jesus Entered Jerusalem   The Last Supper   The Garden of Gethsemane

Grapevine Studies
New Testament

Final Review
Level 1-2

New Testament Timeline

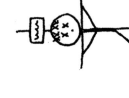
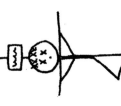
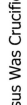

| Jesus Was Arrested | Jesus Tried and Condemned | Jesus Was Crucified | Jesus Died and Was Buried |

3 Religious
3 Civil

SP 201

Grapevine Studies
New Testament

Final Review
Level 1-2

New Testament Timeline

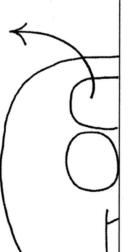
Jesus Rose from the Dead

Jesus Appeared for 40 Days

Jesus Ascended

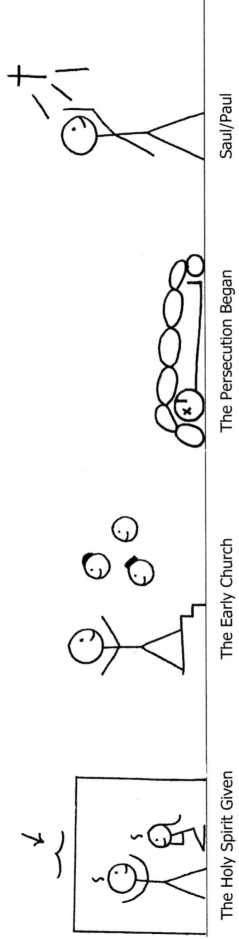

Grapevine Studies
New Testament

Final Review
Level 1-2

New Testament Timeline

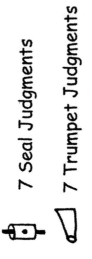

- 7 Seal Judgments
- 7 Trumpet Judgments
- 7 Bowl Judgments

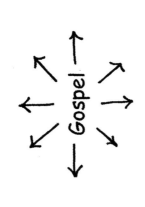

| Letters to the Churches | The Gospel Spreads | The Great Tribulation |

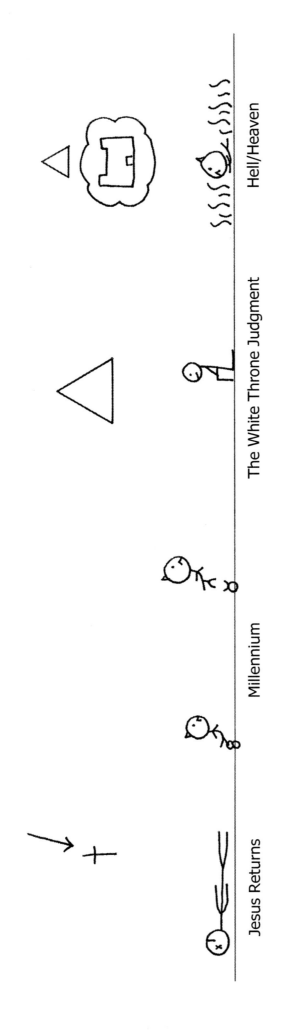

Grapevine Studies
New Testament

Final Review
Level 2

Final Review

Recite or write the following verses on a separate sheet of paper.

1. Luke 1:80
2. Galatians 4:4-5
3. Matthew 2:11
4. Luke 2:52
5. Mark 1:9
6. Hebrews 4:15
7. Revelation 20:10
8. Matthew 28:19-20
9. Matthew 22:37-39
10. Mark 1:35
11. Matthew 8:27
12. Luke 9:16
13. Matthew 4:23
14. Luke 9:1
15. Luke 7:15
16. Matthew 21:9
17. John 13:1
18. Mark 14:36
19. Matthew 26:57
20. Matthew 27:26
21. Luke 23:33
22. Luke 23:46
23. John 19:41-42
24. Mark 16:19
25. John 1:14
26. John 20:30-31
27. Acts 1:8
28. Acts 2:42
29. Acts 7:59
30. Acts 9:15-16
31. II Timothy 4:7-8
32. II Timothy 3:16-17
33. Romans 15:4
34. Matthew 24:14
35. James 1:22
36. Revelation 5:9
37. Revelation 9:20
38. Revelation 1:7
39. Revelation 20:15
40. Revelation 21:3

2005

SP 207

Addendum

The Apostle's Creed

I believe in God, the Father almighty,

creator of heaven and earth.

I believe in Jesus Christ, God's only Son, our Lord,

who was conceived by the Holy Spirit,

born of the Virgin Mary,

suffered under Pontius Pilate,

was crucified, died, and was buried;

he descended to the dead.

On the third day he rose again;

he ascended into heaven,

he is seated at the right hand of the Father,

and he will come again to judge the living and the dead.

I believe in the Holy Spirit,

the holy catholic church,

the communion of saints,

the forgiveness of sins,

the resurrection of the body,

and the life everlasting. AMEN.

Notes for the Apostle's Creed

Weekly Schedule

Week 1 & 2	Lesson 1	Week 28	Lesson 22
Week 3	Lesson 2	Week 29	Lesson 23
Week 4	Lesson 3	Week 30	Lesson 24
Week 5	Lesson 4	Week 31	Review 4
Week 6	Lesson 5	Week 32	Lesson 25
Week 7	Lesson 6	Week 33	Lesson 26
Week 8	Review 1	Week 34	Lesson 27
Week 9	Lesson 7	Week 35	Lesson 28
Week 10	Lesson 8	Week 36	Lesson 29
Week 11	Lesson 9	Week 37	Review 5
Week 12	Lesson 10	Week 38	Lesson 30
Week 13	Lesson 11	Week 39	Lesson 31
Week 14	Lesson 12	Week 40	Lesson 32
Week 15	Review 2	Week 41	Lesson 33
Week 16	Lesson 13	Week 42	Lesson 34
Week 17	Lesson 14	Week 43	Review 6
Week 18	Lesson 15	Week 44	Lesson 35
Week 19	Lesson 16	Week 45	Lesson 36
Week 20	Lesson 17	Week 46	Lesson 37
Week 21	Lesson 18	Week 47	Lesson 38
Week 22	Review 3	Week 48	Lesson 39
Week 23	Mid-Term Review	Week 49	Review 7
Week 24	Mid-Term Review	Week 50	Final Review
Week 25	Lesson 19	Week 51	Final Review
Week 26	Lesson 20	Week 52	FREE
Week 27	Lesson 21		

Weekly Schedule Notes

Daily Schedule

Day 1-4 (Level 3)	Lesson 1
Day 1-3 (Level 4)	Lesson 1
Day 4 (Level 4)	Lesson 2 Quest Page
Day 5	Lesson 2 page 1
Day 6	Lesson 2 page 2
Day 7	Cards and Quest
Day 8	Lesson 3 Review page
Day 9	Lesson 3 page 1
Day 10	Lesson 3 page 2
Day 11	Cards and Quest
Day 12	Lesson 4 Review page
Day 13	Lesson 4 page 1
Day 14	Lesson 4 page 2
Day 15	Cards and Quest
Day 16	Lesson 5 Review page
Day 17	Lesson 5 page 1
Day 18	Lesson 5 page 2
Day 19	Cards and Quest
Day 20	Lesson 6 Review page
Day 21	Lesson 6 page 1
Day 22	Lesson 6 page 2
Day 23-24	Review 1
Day 25	Cards and Quest
Day 26	Lesson 7 Review page
Day 27	Lesson 7 page 1
Day 28	Lesson 7 page 2
Day 29	Cards and Quest
Day 30	Lesson 8 Review page
Day 31	Lesson 8 page 1
Day 32	Lesson 8 page 2
Day 33	Cards and Quest
Day 34	Lesson 9 Review page
Day 35	Lesson 9 page 1
Day 36	Lesson 9 page 2
Day 37	Cards and Quest
Day 38	Lesson 10 Review page
Day 39	Lesson 10 page 1
Day 40	Lesson 10 page 2
Day 41	Cards and Quest
Day 42	Lesson 11 Review page
Day 43	Lesson 11 page 1
Day 44	Lesson 11 page 2
Day 45	Cards and Quest
Day 46	Lesson 12 Review page
Day 47	Lesson 12 page 1
Day 48	Lesson 12 page 2
Day 49-50	Review 2
Day 51	Cards and Quest
Day 52	Lesson 13 Review page
Day 53	Lesson 13 page 1
Day 54	Lesson 13 page 2
Day 55	Cards and Quest
Day 56	Lesson 14 Review page
Day 57	Lesson 14 page 1
Day 58	Lesson 14 page 2
Day 59	Cards and Quest
Day 60	Lesson 15 Review page
Day 61	Lesson 15 page 1
Day 62	Lesson 15 page 2
Day 63	Cards and Quest
Day 64	Lesson 16 Review page
Day 65	Lesson 16 page 1
Day 66	Lesson 16 page 2
Day 67	Cards and Quest
Day 68	Lesson 17 Review page
Day 69	Lesson 17 page 1
Day 70	Lesson 17 page 2
Day 71	Cards and Quest
Day 72	Lesson 18 Review page
Day 73	Lesson 18 page 1
Day 74	Lesson 18 page 2
Day 75-76	Review 3
Day 77-78	Mid-Term Review
Day 79	Cards and Quest
Day 80	Lesson 19 Review page
Day 81	Lesson 19 page 1
Day 82	Lesson 19 page 2
Day 83	Cards and Quest
Day 84	Lesson 20 Review page
Day 85	Lesson 20 page 1
Day 86	Lesson 20 page 2

Day 87	Cards and Quest
Day 88	Lesson 21 Review page
Day 89	Lesson 21 page 1
Day 90	Lesson 21 page 2
Day 91	Cards and Quest
Day 92	Lesson 22 Review page
Day 93	Lesson 22 page 1
Day 94	Lesson 22 page 2
Day 95	Cards and Quest
Day 96	Lesson 23 Review page
Day 97	Lesson 23 page 1
Day 98	Lesson 23 page 2
Day 99-100	Review 4
Day 101	Cards and Quest
Day 102	Lesson 24 Review page
Day 103	Lesson 24 page 1
Day 104	Lesson 24 page 2
Day 105	Cards and Quest
Day 106	Lesson 25 Review page
Day 107	Lesson 25 page 1
Day 108	Lesson 25 page 2
Day 109	Cards and Quest
Day 110	Lesson 26 Review page
Day 111	Lesson 26 page 1
Day 112	Lesson 26page 2
Day 113	Cards and Quest
Day 114	Lesson 27 Review page
Day 115	Lesson 27 page 1
Day 116	Lesson 27 page 2
Day 117	Cards and Quest
Day 118	Lesson 28 Review page
Day 119	Lesson 28 page 1
Day 120	Lesson 28 page 2
Day 121	Cards and Quest
Day 122	Lesson 29 Review page
Day 123	Lesson 29 page 1
Day 124	Lesson 29 page 2
Day 125-126	Review 5
Day 127	Cards and Quest
Day 128	Lesson 30 Review page
Day 129	Lesson 30 page 1
Day 130	Lesson 30 page 2
Day 131	Cards and Quest
Day 132	Lesson 31 Review page
Day 133	Lesson 31 page 1
Day 134	Lesson 31 page 2
Day 135	Cards and Quest
Day 136	Lesson 32 Review page
Day 137	Lesson 32 page 1
Day 138	Lesson 32 page 2
Day 139	Cards and Quest
Day 140	Lesson 33 Review page
Day 141	Lesson 33 page 1
Day 142	Lesson 33 page 2
Day 143	Cards and Quest
Day 144	Lesson 34 Review page
Day 145	Lesson 34 page 1
Day 146	Lesson 34 page 2
Day 147-148	Review 6
Day 149	Cards and Quest
Day 150	Lesson 35 Review page
Day 151	Lesson 35 page 1
Day 152	Lesson 35 page 2
Day 153	Cards and Quest
Day 154	Lesson 36 Review page
Day 155	Lesson 36 page 1
Day 156	Lesson 36 page 2
Day 157	Cards and Quest
Day 158	Lesson 37 Review page
Day 159	Lesson 37 page 1
Day 160	Lesson 37 page 2
Day 161	Cards and Quest
Day 162	Lesson 38 Review page
Day 163	Lesson 38 page 1
Day 164	Lesson 38 page 2
Day 165	Cards and Quest
Day 166	Lesson 39 Review page
Day 167	Lesson 39 page 1
Day 168	Lesson 39 page 2
Day 169-170	Review 7
Day 171-175	Final Review

Congratulations on your completion of the New Testament Overview!

Continue your journey through the Bible with the Level 1 Old Testament Overview!

Students will learn:
- The Old Testament Timeline
- Basic Old Testament Geography
- See how Jesus restores the broken relationship between God and man.
- Learn about the people, events, and places of the Old Testament.

Continue your journey through the Bible with the Level 2 Old Testament Overview!

Students will learn:
- The Old Testament Timeline
- Learn where the Old Testament books fit in chronologically, who wrote the books, and to whom were they written.
- See how Jesus restores the broken relationship between God and man.
- Continue to master the use of Bible study tools.

Order your
Old Testament Overview Course
Today!

By Phone
877-436-2317

On Line
www.grapevinestudies.com

Recommended Resources from Grapevine Studies

Student Bible Atlas

This colorful atlas includes 30 maps that will give your students a clear understanding of where biblical events took place. Your student will be able to trace the journeys of Abraham, cross the Red Sea with Moses and follow the missionary journeys of Paul.

Atlas of the Holy Lands

Older students will enjoy this wonderfully illustrated atlas which includes 80 maps, helpful illustrations, archaeological information thematic maps and much more! Your student will be able to use this atlas to make their Bible study come to life.

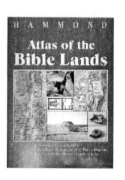

Every student needs basic Bible study resources: a Concordance, Bible Dictionary, and Topical Bible. Your student will find these concise and conveniently sized resources perfect for their first references! Teachers can also use this 3 book set for gifts or prizes!

Order Today!

By Phone
877-436-2317

On Line
www.grapevinestudies.com

Grapevine Studies Curriculums

Old and New Testament Overview Books

Beginner (Ages 5-7)
Beginner students will enjoy this hands-on study of the major characters and events of the Bible using simple, colorful stick figures, and symbols. Teachers will appreciate the chronological and easy-to-teach format! At the end of the year your students will have learned 40+ memory verses and will have created their first Bible study resource book! One-year study.

Level 1 (Grades 1-2)
Level 1 students will begin to learn the Old or New Testament Timeline, with each subsequent lesson related to a point on the timeline. Teachers will see measurable results in just a few lessons! In one year your students should be able to recite 38+ memory verses, fill out the timeline and tell you several facts about each character or event on the timeline. One-year study.

Level 2 (Grades 3-4)
Level 2 students will expand their knowledge of the Bible timeline while learning new facts about each timeline character and event. Memory work includes the books of the Bible in order and by category. One-year study.
   Old Testament memory work: Ten Commandments and the Twelve Sons of Jacob.
   New Testament Memory work: Twelve Apostles and the Apostle's Creed.

Level 3 (Grades 5-8)
Level 3 students will deepen their understanding of the Old or New Testament characters and events. Students should be able to complete either the Old or New Testament Timeline on their own. In addition, students will be introduced to basic biblical geography, so they will not only know what happened but where it happened! One-year study.

Level 4 (Teen-Adult)
Level 4 students will master the Old or New Testament Timeline and know where the books of the Bible fit into the chronology of the Timeline. Students will also be introduced to and practice using basic Bible study tools: a Bible Concordance, A Bible Dictionary, and a Topical Bible with each lesson. Students will also be challenged with critical thinking questions associated with each lesson. One-year study.

Level 5 (Teen-Adult)
Take a self-directed approach to studying the Old or New Testament. Students will take notes, use Bible study resources, and answer critical thinking questions in each lesson. Hands-on activities and research projects make this an excellent study for students who desire to move to deepen their understanding of the Bible. Start your study today! No teacher manuals needed. One-year study.

Biblical Feasts and Holy Days Study

Learn what God expected from His people when they celebrated and observed the feasts and holy days. Discover how Jesus has fulfilled the spring feasts with His first appearance. Read about what New Testament events that occurred on or around the feasts and holy days. This study will give you a better understanding of the New Testament and all that Jesus did for us. Begin your 13 week study today! *Available in both the Stick Figure curriculum and Blueprint curriculum.*

Congratulations on your completion of the Old Testament Overview! We, at Grapevine Studies, pray that this study has been a blessing to you and your students! We would love to hear from you!!

Send your comments to:

Email

info@grapevinestudies.com

Snail mail

PO Box 2123
Glenrock, WY 82637-2123

Order your
New Testament Overview Course
Today!

Website

www.grapevinestudies.com